Classifi

Revelations From The Father

Xavier Dequane
Scott

For information contact :
(CB49192@gmail.com)

Book and Cover design by Xavier Dequane Scott

First Edition : Month 2017

10 9 8 7 6 5 4 3 2 1

THE CONTENTS

Prayer for Salvation

Prayer of Salvation - Our First Real Conversation with God

The "prayer of salvation" is the most important prayer we'll ever pray. When we're ready to become a Christian, we're ready to have our first real conversation with God, and these are its components:

• We acknowledge that Jesus Christ is God; that He came to earth as a man in order to live the sinless life that we cannot live; that He died in our place, so that we would not have to pay the penalty we deserve.

• We confess our past life of sin -- living for ourselves and not obeying God.

• We admit we are ready to trust Jesus Christ as our Savior and Lord.

• We ask Jesus to come into our heart, take up residence there, and begin living through us.

Prayer of Salvation - It Begins with Faith in God

When we pray the prayer of salvation, we're letting God know we believe His Word is true. By the faith He has given us, we choose to believe in Him. The Bible tells us that "*without faith it is impossible to please Him, for he who comes to God must believe that He is, and that He is a rewarder of those who diligently seek Him*" ***(Hebrews 11:6)***. So, when we pray, asking God for the gift of salvation, we're exercising our free will to acknowledge that we believe in Him. That demonstration of faith pleases God, because we have freely chosen to know Him.

Prayer of Salvation - Confessing Our Sin

When we pray the prayer of salvation, we're admitting that we've sinned. As the Bible says of everyone, save Christ alone: *"For all have sinned, and fall short of the glory of God"* ***(Romans 3:23)***. To sin is simply to fall short of the mark, as an arrow that does not quite hit the bull's-eye. The glory of God that we fall short of is found only in Jesus Christ: "For it is the God who commanded light to shine out of darkness, who has shone in our hearts to give the light of the knowledge of the glory of God in the face of Jesus Christ" ***(2 Corinthians 4:6)***. The prayer of salvation, then, recognizes that Jesus Christ is the only human who ever lived without sin. "For He made Him who knew no sin to be sin for us, that we might become the righteousness of God in Him" ***(2 Corinthians 5:21)***.

Prayer of Salvation - Professing Faith in Christ as Savior

With Christ as our standard of perfection, we're now acknowledging faith in Him as God, agreeing with the Apostle John that: *"In the beginning was the Word (Christ), and the Word was with God, and the Word was God. He was in the beginning with God. All things were made through Him, and without Him nothing was made that was made"***(John 1:1-3).** Because God could only accept a perfect, sinless sacrifice, and because He knew that we could not possibly accomplish that, He sent His Son to die for us and pay the eternal price. *"For God so loved the world that He gave His only begotten Son, that whoever believes in Him should not perish but have everlasting life."* ***(John 3:16)***. Do you agree with everything you have read so far? If you do, don't wait a moment longer to start your new life in Jesus Christ. Remember, this prayer is not a magical formula. You are simply expressing your heart to God. Pray this with us: "Father, I know that I have broken your laws and my sins have separated me from you. I am truly sorry, and now I want to turn away from my past sinful life toward you. Please forgive me, and help me avoid sinning again. I believe that your son, Jesus Christ died for my sins, was resurrected from the dead, is alive, and hears my prayer. I invite Jesus to become the Lord of my life, to rule and reign in my heart from this day forward. Amen." If you've said that prayer you've been born again but in order to be confirmed into the image of Christ you have to have the Holy Spirit and in order to get the Holy Spirit you have to get baptized in water. If you don't know the purpose of the Holy Spirit the Holy Spirit is a helper sent from God to help you and teach you how to live holy like Jesus. It says it in John chapter four in verse twenty-six. Not only is he there to keep you holy he's there to communicate to you the promises of God and what God wants to use you for. How do you know that you have the Holy Spirit? You'll feel a warmness in your back, stomach or chest and it feels like an authentic love or peace that you've never experience before. You may speak in tongues, you may not but don't worry if you don't that's not the only manifestation of the Holy Spirit because he works through us in different ways. You can read 1st Corinthians chapter twelve from verse seven through verse eleven that talks about the manifestations of the Holy Spirit.

- No such thing as once saved always saved (You get saved and go back to sin that's an no no bro you must work out your salvation with fear and trembling) You need to be in constant fellowship with God in order to stay in the Spirit so you won't fulfill the lust of your stinking flesh (Galatians 5:19-23) If you sin again just repent and confess your sin before the throne of God and he'll cleanse you from all unrighteousness (1st John 1:9)

- You're self-will is gone also once you get saved so basically you don't have an say anymore it's either God's will or not. If you don't choose God's will it's ok, you'll still be saved but 10/10 he won't bless what you want to do because he already has a plan for your life before the foundations of the world. (Jeremiah 1:5 / 29:11) For I know the plans I have for you," declares the Lord, "plans to prosper you and not to harm you, plans to give you hope and a future." Those who do the will of God after they die will receive the crown of life when they get to heaven and multiple rewards.

Introduction of this book

The meaning of this book titled “Classified revelations from the Father” means Hidden revelations from The MOST HIGH YHWH (The LORD) and I wrote this book during a time period when I was most intimate with God during my wilderness seasons and God was opening up to me deep revelations about scripture that I’m going to unveil to you the hidden revelations about what the LORD told me about HIS Holy Word. All praises go to TMH for helping me write this book to my fellow brethren.

CHAPTER ONE

How did I become a Christian???

When I was younger, I was raised in a Christian home of course ever since I was born. I was born in the state of South Carolina and lived in a city called Columbia all of my life. Like most people, I loved the Lord and went to church every Sunday but that made me thought that I was in right standing with him because I did those religious things and that wasn't the case at all because, in my eyes and in my parent's eyes, I was 'good' when in reality I was still operating under the sin nature despite how many good things I've done for people. You know just like everyone else I still dealt with my own struggles and heartaches and with me growing up with an optimistic personality and good character. That's how I overcame most of my struggles but most of all it was God who was on my side now that I look back on it, I didn't know that the Lord instilled those traits in me to predestine me to become the Christian that I am right now. During those days, I was still going to church and reading the bible religiously because my grandparents said so. I still didn't know what it was like to encounter God or the love of God. I didn't know what it was like to be cleansed from sin because every time that I'd sinned, I'll feel dirty and repent religiously not noticing that I was still a sinner and I didn't have salvation or the blood of Jesus to help me cleanse my sin. Instead, I thought that I was still in right standing with the Lord because I prayed, went to church, read the bible, and did good works to make me feel good about myself not noticing again that I was still a sinner and that I needed the salvation of Jesus Christ. Some people who were born into church and who were raised and taught by the principles of the bible tend to believe that they're in right standing with God because they do all of those religious things and practices while a person who's in sin know that they're not in right standing with God and they know that they're not worthy of him so they ask him for mercy and forgiveness for their trust passes. I'm not saying that my life was perfect or that I was perfect, but what I'm trying to say is there's a difference between a sinner who was raised in church and who knows the bible versus a sinner who didn't grow up in church and who doesn't know the bible. The sinner who grew up in church is more responsible than the sinner who didn't grew up in church and who doesn't know the bible. This is why ***(2 Peter 2:21)*** tells us that, "*for it is better for a person to not know the truth than to know it and to turn away from the Lord's commandments and disobey him.*" The sinner or the Christian who knows the bible are more responsible than the sinner who doesn't know because the truth of God's word was revealed to them.

God will curse you if you do that because that's a part of his spiritual law. That's like seeing a sci-fi or horror movie where the superhero shows an average everyday person their true identity, signs and wonders then afterwards the person who was shown the signs and wonders by that superhero told everybody in the county or city about what the superhero did and now everybody around town knows about it and now the person who first saw the superhero behind the mask true identity and they saw the superhero perform the signs and the wonders are now held accountable for the secret being revealed out in the open. This gives baby Christians and sinners who don't know the word of God the ok to live how you want to live and to sin how long you want to sin especially if it's a sinner who wants to get converted into the Christian faith; so when a sinner do come to the faith, they can discards God's word and go right back into sin because they saw a Christian or a sinner who knew the word of God do it thinking that they're still going to be in the Lord when they do that and that's not the case at all. Whoever believes that believes in the false doctrine "once saved always saved". Number one, you're not saved until you endure towards the end, number two, you don't have salvation until you apply faith towards it and your works will follow and last but not least you have to work out your own salvation with fear and trembling that means being in the word of God, repenting and refraining from sin, praying and fasting, and staying in fellowship with Christians who have the same faith and spiritual frequency as you and I will get on the topic of fellowshipping with other Christians and what fellowship really means in the third chapter. Getting back on topic!!! I didn't know God personally or I didn't know him from a spiritual and relational standpoint because in my head I thought that he was just God and you do this and don't do that or you'll go to hell etc. That was my mindset of God until I got saved on Mother's Day in the year of twenty-fourteen. Before I discuss my journey with the Lord after I got saved I want to tell you about my life and how I was before I got saved. Like I said in the beginning of the book I was raised in church and I was brought up on Christian values and beliefs, but I had my own struggles and problems just like any other sinner before they came to the Lord has had. Growing up I had an easy life but I didn't have an easy life and the reason why I say this is because of the way that I was raised and how I was brought up. I did have an easy life when it came down to materialistic things and not lacking any food, shelter, and clothes but that wasn't the issue; the issue was how I got those things. When I was younger during my elementary stages my mom would be struggling working two jobs while my dad would sell drugs in order to make ends meet. Now my father wasn't always like that because he grew up in a middle-class home but ever since his mother died (my grandmother) his dad (my grandfather) went through a depression stage and didn't want to provide at that time for my dad so my father had to make his own way for his provision which was selling drugs and from that point on that was his occupation. So basically, from the time I was walking and towards the time of elementary stages I had Jordan's stacked up in my closet due to my father's drug dealing. My mom would help me out and give me stuff as well but at least it was the legal way. When I went to school during my elementary stages I had worn most clothing brands than most of my peers: wearing Rockefeller jackets, shirts, Nikes and Jordan's while they would come to school dressed up in uniforms. Comparing to the knowledge that I had back then to the spiritual wisdom that I have known that the Rockefellers are a part of the elite and that what I was wearing was a part of the occult but at the time I didn't know that because YouTube wasn't around back then, I was in the world, and every worldly person seemed to like that trend so to me I thought that it was good to wear because other people had liked it but now that the Lord has revealed to me that their clothing line was linked to satan and his kingdom I no longer care about clothing and the trends of this world because every clothing that they put out is demonic. During those times, I use to put my worth and my self-esteem in the way I dressed, looked, and appeared to other people and I seriously thought that would bring me true fulfillment in life when none of those things would continue to appease me. Not only did I have a good childhood to where the kids at school had liked my clothing and the way that I dress but I also had bad childhood moments as well. I would have fights in school, act out in class, and get bad grades in school as a result of not getting enough attention and love that I need at home the only love that I did get was from my mother but my father only showed me love when it came down to materialistic things but he was aggressive when it came down to my grades and to how I was behaving in school. As a result of my father selling drugs, not having to experience the love and care of his mother, and not having a father to care for him like he did that made him aggressive and he had zero tolerance for stupidity and foolishness. Every time I would make a mistake, make bad grades, or I couldn't understand something he would at first verbally abuse me and call me all kinds of names, then he would physically abuse me and call me more names on top of that and sometimes my mother would come home from work and catch me bruised up and get on my father about it and the next thing you know they would get into it and I have to witness my mother getting physically abused by him and just take it because I was little and I couldn't do anything about it during that stage of my life. Due to the physical abuse and the dysfunction that was going on inside of our home at that time caused me to develop a bad case of social anxiety and trauma. I didn't like people because I thought that everyone was the same and I felt that every man that I encountered as a boy I thought that they would treat me the same as my father did because of how he made me feel. Sometimes I feel like if you're around a crazy or dysfunctional person for way too long you will become like that person which is more than likely to be true but it doesn't have to necessarily be the truth. Yeah, I may have growed up in a dysfunctional family but now that I know the truth (which is the word of God) and I know that I am a new creature in Christ and I am to become the image of Jesus Christ I now know that I don't have to stay bound to the old man or to my past because of the new identity that the Lord has given me. I can either choose to follow old family tradition or I can apply the word of God in my life and listen to what my Creator says about how to live the righteous way versus taking on man's wisdom and carrying on family tradition. You have a choice to do those two things if you're a Christian; sinners only take on worldly advice and family tradition because they operate under a carnal mind and the carnal mind can only operate under experience and reasoning (which is demonic because that's how Satan works.) This is why the word of God tells us that <u>*the carnal man is emity against God.*</u> ***(Romans 8:7)*** The word also tells us to refrain from ungodly counseling and advice; but to apply the word of God and walk according to what he says over what the world says in ***(Psalms 1:1-6)***. If you do be a friend of the world and take their ungodly counseling and advice it's a curse when you do that you will not prosper because <u>*if you're a friend of the world you are an enemy of God.*</u> ***(James 4:4)***. This is why when you talk about spiritual things carnal people who are still in the world can't understand you because they've been blinded by the father of lies and they're operating under a different dimension than Christians are. When they're under a carnal mindset they're operating from below the earth which is the deepest and darkest dimension (which is satan's kingdom) but when a Christian is operating from a spiritual mindset or a renewed mind as one would say you're operating from above (above-meaning the heavens and below meaning the earth realm.) Remember in my third book where I talked about in the second chapter where satan mentions the meaning *as above so below*, and I said that the meaning was a satanic philosophy twisted and it was originally called on *earth as it is in heaven* which was made by God the Creator himself. When you hear the meaning 'As above so below' it means that whatever is taken place in the underworld (or the marine kingdom which is satan's kingdom) will manifest in the natural realm (or earth realm) as materialism and circumstances. It's the same thing with Christians whatever we have faith towards in the spirit and we walk it out by faith it'll manifest in the natural as well. A lot of Christians don't know what happens when they are befriending the world especially when the Lord told them to come out of the world because for one, the matrix isn't real it's all an illusion, and number two satan's kingdom is on earth and we should know that the earth isn't our natural habitat because our home is in heaven, this is why we feel uncomfortable and we feel like we don't belong here and sometimes we feel that we want to be home with the Lord because the earth isn't our spiritual home we're just put here on the earth to be used by God as a vessel of honor to accomplish his work and his assignment to manifest his kingdom in the earth realm. Before you are born God has already set up the life that he wants you to have he just allow you to get messed up so that you can run to him and that's the situation that I was in. The Lord already predestine me to become a service of honor for his kingdom I just didn't know it. I knew that I was mostly nice, kind, and laidback despite my upbringing but I didn't necessarily know why I was born this way. I think during my elementary stages of my life I was ministering to a girl name Naddia in the first grade at the playground about her life and what she went through and ever since then I always want to help people but because of my upbringing I didn't like people and when I came to the Lord he had to purge me of the hate that was in me because of my past and the way that I was brought up. In a sense when you do come to the faith you already know that you were handpicked by God because you're already different and you don't fit in with people so in a way you can say that the Lord has already predestine me for the destiny that he wants me to fulfill I was just in the process of carrying out the agenda that he wants me to accomplish. And guess what God's using me to minister to the broken, to the people who's been cast away, and looked down on and I'm not going to lie sometimes it's frustrating but I can do all things through Christ who strengthens me. It's not about me it's about the Lord and what he wants me to accomplish while I'm still on this earth, and when I'm done he'll take me out. During my middle school days, I finally found my voice and how to deal with the pain that I was bearing through writing and dancing. During my teenage years, I started to get out of my shell but for all of you true readers out there you should know that during my first book I told you about the person that the Lord has used to push me out of my shell and her name was Ms. Stackhouse. For all of you who aren't familiar with her she was my resource teacher and she helped God create the person who he saw when I came out of my mother's womb and I will elaborate on this topic more after I give you guys scripture. The book of Jeremiah talks about this and I can relate to Jeremiah in a way because we both were insecure at some point and with Jeremiah's situation, he couldn't talk but the Lord still used Jeremiah for his purpose. ***(Jeremiah 1:5)*** *"Before I formed you in the womb I knew you, before you were born I set you apart; I appointed you as a prophet to the nations"* Before I was born God appointed me to be a servant for his kingdom just like Jeremiah was and he predestine my life way before I came into the world. This is how I knew!!! When I was four years old I had the gift of writing and this is how I knew that I had the gift of writing. One day my dad brought me a type - writer and I taught myself how to write because it automatically came natural for me. On the floor, I had fifty sheets of paper wrapped up in a package and I tore the package up, putting a sheet of paper in between the typewriter's paper table and the platen, turned the knob on the side of the roller to keep the paper well-grounded so it won't fall when I started typing. Ever since then I loved writing!!! I would even write during my teenage years to cope with the pain that I was dealing with due to the abuse and dysfunction that was happening in my home. I would have countless of journals written full of poems, stories, songs, and other kinds of written material and I would keep them wrapped in a grocery store bag in a drawer where nobody would find them because I didn't want anyone to know that I was hurting. Until one day I meet a lady that completely changed my life and she was clearly God ordained now that I look back over my life. That was God's sovereignty and her name was Ms. Stackhouse!!! During my teenage years when I was in middle school, while I was in her class she would make me feel so special (which I wasn't used to feeling that way) and you know people with the spirit of rejection are used to people criticizing them and making them feel inferior due to the lack of love they never had and the unstable environment that they were in. I still kind of struggle with the spirit of rejection but not the way I use to though. But when I met Ms. Stackhouse, everything had changed!!! She made me feel like family even though I wasn't her biological family by blood I was her family by association and God's sovereignty. On a special day when we finished our classes we would throw down in her class and what I mean by throw down we would have fun. We would play music until school was over, and of course when I was a teenager, she knew that I loved listening to Michael Jackson and we would play all of his music and I'd be dancing to every one of his songs. Not only did we listen to music we also had some food. I'm not talking about some ordinary food that you get from the canteen or from the cafeteria I'm talking about some real food or as black people like to call it 'soul food'. We had some mac and cheese, fried chicken, shrimp alfredo, nachos with chili and cheese, two varieties of cheese cakes: One was an oreo cheese cake and the other was a strawberry cheese cake. We also had ceaser salad's and some hotdogs and burgers that were cooked on

the grill. God bless that woman and I thanked Jesus for her. I had eaten about almost everything in that class because I was born with a high metabolism. Thank Jesus for that too!!! It's very rare that you find a teacher that actually care about their students nowadays because teacher nowadays only care about the money. Ms. Stackhouse pushed me to my potential and brought me out of my shyness because God wanted to use her as a vessel of honor to create in me what he saw in me when he pre-ordained me before I came into this world. I remember later during my middle school days she recommended me to try taking dance classes since I loved dancing to Michael Jackson so much and I agreed to her request and boy did I tell you I felt like I was Michael Jackson among the four brothers that were in the same class that I was in. When I took dance classes of course they had females in the class but there were also what I like to consider 'The Jackson five' in the classroom as well. It was me of course, Jacob, Eddie, Alezea, and Raqwan.
One of our rehearsals were the five of us during our part of the routine in the song ***"Waiting on the world to change"*** by- John Mayer while the girls had their part of the song so when it was time to do our part of the song we at first had our guy routine until our dance instructor recommended that we included the girls in our part of the dance routine and back then I was just like any other teenager I loved me some females and when you're in the world it seemed natural and attractive but now that I've come into the realization of my spiritual identity in Christ it's not attractive because that's

lust and it's carnal and ***(Proverbs 6:25)*** tells us to *not lust after a woman in your heart neither let her take thee with her eyelids.* If you do lust over a woman it can lead to destruction and it says this in (***Proverbs 7:1-27)***. Being a born-again creature in Christ Jesus we are attracted to the spirit of God in a person not the fleshly attributes on a person. We are to be led by the Holy Spirit in all things just like ***(Romans 8:14)*** tells us to. If God didn't lead you to this person whether it be male or female and he hasn't revealed to you who your spouse is then looking at another person like that especially if it's a Christian is lust and perversion. ***(1 Timothy 5:1-2)*** Now let's resume back to the story!!! We rehearsed for the dance concert for about four weeks so after the four weeks was over the concert was due. Normally you'd think that I'll be ready for a concert after four weeks of rehearsing but due to the anxiety that I was feeling I wasn't ready even though the boys and the rest of the dance crew was ready. In the locker room, I was jittery and nervous because I never performed in front of a huge crowd so my boys were trying to calm me down and I wasn't saved then so I couldn't cast those evil thoughts down like the word of God tells us to because I wasn't in covenant with the Lord before I got saved and the word tells us that *God doesn't hear the prayers of sinners.* ***(John 9:31)*** So I applied what I learned when I was in the world, "The man up" tactic. When it was time for us to perform, I felt like I was ready and I killed that dance routine. After that I felt confident but it was a false sense of confidence outside of God and it was a confidence builted off of the world and personal insecurity now that I think about it. So, as we kept doing the concerts and the dance routine my "confidence" was in my talent and my own abilities. I had that mindset of, "If other people liked me and my talent than I like myself." Kind of mindset!!! I was a people's pleaser and I was under people's bondage. Now that I'm saved I live to please the Lord now and I'm not living to please man anymore. Just like Paul had said in ***(Galatians 1:10)*** "*Am I now trying to win the approval of human beings, or of God? Or am I trying to please people? If I were still trying to please people, I would not be a servant of Christ.*" What can man do for you at the end of the day? Do they know the thoughts of God's heart towards you? Do they know the plans that he has for you, no because God is my refuge and my strength!!! ***(Psalms 46:1-5)*** *God is our refuge and strength, a very present help in trouble.* [2] *Therefore will not we fear, though the earth be removed, and though the mountains, be carried in the midst of the sea;* [3] *Though the waters thereof roar and be troubled. Though the mountains shake with the swelling thereof. Selah.* [4] There *is a river, the streams whereof shall make glad the city of God, the holy place of the tabernacles of the most High.* [5] *God is in the midst of her; she shall not be moved: God shall help her, and that right early.* Fear no man but the Lord!!! When we got promoted from middle school towards high school and it was time to go to another level in the educational system. I took Ms. Stackhouse's advice with me to ensure success of me getting out of those special-ed classes. During my freshman year in high school I overcame a lot of crazy stuff and it was by the Lord's sovereign hand that any weapon formed against me didn't prosper. During my high school freshman days, I saw: (Fireworks being blasted inside the cafeteria, a lot of fights from students fighting one on one and a lot of people jumping someone in a handicap match, people selling cocaine and trying to shoot up drugs, and food fights going on in the cafeteria etc.) Obviously, all of that didn't get to me because I knew how to maneuver around the drama so that I could go home to my mama (laughs while typing). But one day during my freshman year while attending that school my teacher Ms. Adam told me that I wasn't going to get my high school diploma as long as I stayed in special ed class and I wasn't in agreement with that. God used Ms. Stackhouse so of course she told me differently, she told me that I would get it as long as I stayed working hard focusing on my school work and it did come to pass what she said will come to pass. God is good!!! As I worked hard and focused on my school work during my freshman year it finally paid off during the second quarter of my sophomore year when Ms. Adam finally told me that the hard work I did in her class finally paid off and I was getting released from special ed class and promoted into resource class by the time my third quarter of being a sophomore had begun. The struggle was real!!! Now before my junior year during my sophomore year I paid Ms. Stackhouse a visit just to go up to the middle school to go check up on her and she seemed pretty fine to me from what I knew back then. We sat and chatted and she asked me if I was still taking dance classes I told her that I still was taking them during that time and we chatted about my classes and the progress that I made and when it was time to go I gave her a hug and walk out the classroom and that was the last time I saw her unfortunately. Now after my sophomore year had wrapped up, I was ready for the summer. Then after the summer year had wrapped up, I was a junior in high school then about time that school year was wrapped up I called her for the summer to check up on her and another person had answered the phone. She said, "Hello, hello who is this calling?" I said to her, "My name is Xavier and I'm looking for Ms. Stackhouse." She replied, "Xavier, nice to meet you but I'm sorry to tell you this but Ms. Stackhouse passed away." After I heard her say that I hung up the phone in denial of what the lady said. Ms. Stackhouse aka my second mama passed away on June 6, 2014. Before her death, I'd planned to go see her again earlier in 2014 but I didn't have the chance to and she died shortly afterwards as soon as I got out of special ed classes so that's not a coincidence God was using her to bring out the best in me. That lady had a huge impact on my life and God used that woman tremendously in order to instill something that he wanted in me in order to accomplish His purpose for my life. God bless her soul and I miss her so much. God used her to contribute not only to me graduating high school in 2015 but getting my high school diploma. God is sovereign but during my high school days I had gotten into some stuff as well; I was good when it came to doing school work but when it came time getting out of school, I had gone out with the crew afterschool. (This was way before I got saved by the way.) During my sophomore year, I had met a guy who was in my gym class who first came to the school during the second or third quarter of my sophomore school year and all the girls had liked him because the girls would be feeling his hair and were trying to braid his hair because he had a 1960s afro and that was rare to find so you know the ladies was all over him. One day I went over to talk to him and I told him, “Wassup man I see you getting all the girls.” and he said something like, “Yea brah they be all up on me man who are you?” I told him, “My name is Xavier you can call me Zea for short.” He replied, “My name is Rammelle Freeman but you can call me mel for short.” and we went from there. Every time we get together in the gym, we would play basketball or some other games in the gym. We decided to build our friendship from spending time together in the gym and it escalated into us hanging out in the real world. The first time we hung out was when I was at my grandma house and he showed up with a black BMX bike along with several other friends as well which were Jasmine, and Raqwan and I had a small BMX bike and we rode from my grandmother’s house all the way to Raqwan’s house and we hung out there. We played the game and watched TV. This was when I felt accepted and my mindset started to change but the thing was I was accepted by the wrong people. That first encounter with them changed my life in a bad way and this is what the bible talks about when it says that *bad company corrupts good character* ***(1 Corinthians 15:33)*** It seemed like everything was good and great at first but like my mama said, "everything that glitter ain't gold." When I continued hanging out with them one day, I was at my house I was relaxing about to go somewhere and out of nowhere Rammelle called me because he needed my help with something that he caused. He told me that he needed help trying to come up with bail money before he goes to jail. I agreed and before I had left to go somewhere I went into my closet to get my dominos case (which was full of money I had saved due to me saving money from doing chores around the house.) Rammelle was caught on camera trying to steal soda from outside of a motel when the Indian caught him outside of the motel trying to steal soda, he called the cops and the cops charged them a bail fee and if Jasmine, Raqwan, and Rammelle didn't pay it then the three of them would go to jail. Now my mother was going somewhere so asked her can I go and she said yes so, I decided to go with her I didn't know where we were going at the time but when we passed through churches chicken and the Word of God church I knew that we were going to my grandmother's house. When we pulled up, I gave Rammelle a call and told him where I was at (which was my grandmother's house) and about an hour later he pulled up in his black BMX bike and I gave him the money. He asked me if I was going to go out with him and I told him that my bike tire was flat so I couldn't hang out with him that day. The next time I saw him was when I was at Jasmine's house and he was over there picking cans trying to make more money to come up with the rest of the bail money so that the both of them wouldn't go to jail. While I was sitting on the porch at Jasmine's house Jasmine told me what had happened and I knew that what they were involved in was a red flag for me to stop hanging out with them but I continued anyway because I felt obligated to be there. They pulled through and didn't go to jail because I did my part. After my visit, something was telling me to quit hanging out with them but I refused and I kept on hanging out with them because I didn't want to be alone. At that time, I was struggling with the spirit of rejection so I did what I had to do in order to be accepted by them because I wanted to be accepted so bad. I was going through an identity crisis. This was way before I got saved. Every time I would hang out with Jasmine we would go hang out in her house and play the PS3 and after that we would roll up a joint and get high in the back of her backyard inside one of her mom's old car with the windows rolled up. We would be cracking up jokes inside the car, watching videos on the phone, teasing each other, and laughing out loud for no reason. Weed is sorcery and sorcery is witchcraft. The same weed that people smoke today was used in the biblical times in order to perform rituals and to become one with evil demonic spirits in the spiritual realm. If you're saved and you smoke weed then weed brings down your spiritual covering and it allows demons to enter into your mind in order to dumb you down and to gain access to your mind and if the enemy has your mind then he has you. What we get the word pharmacy from is in the Greek which means *'pharmakia'* and the Greek word *'pharmakia'* means sorcery and sorcery means witchcraft and voodoo. That same day I was hanging out with them I drunk a bottle of vodka as well and I never been the same afterwards. I felt good for the moment, but when I got home and went to sleep, I had a huge headache. My attitude changed towards my mother and I would get an attitude with her and at the time I didn't know that it was an evil spirit using me to do that to her because I was spiritually blinded. And ***(2 Corinthians 4:4)*** tells us that, *Satan has blinded the minds of those who don't believe the gospel of Jesus Christ.* The more I hanged out with the "bad guys" the more invincible I felt. Not only were they stealing sodas and small stuff but they were breaking into people's houses and stealing stuff as well and when I got comfortable with them I knew about it but I still kept them around because I wanted to feel secured and protected around them because of the insecurity that I was feeling. I grew up around drug dealers, hustlers, and gang members but I didn't want to be associated with them because my dad wanted me to have a better life than what he had experienced despite the up's and down's that we had. He taught me to be a leader and not a follower and that's one thing I can't say that he didn't taught me. During that time, clearly, I was being a follower because I thought that was normal because of what I was exposed to when I was a young kid. Like I said I grewed up in church and I knew what I was doing was wrong but I didn't reap the consequences till one day I felt the heaviness of the sin that I was carrying on my shoulder and I got depressed. I noticed that I wasn't my usual self anymore because of who I was around. Now I know that bad company does corrupt good character but I was a good person out of my own righteousness instead of the Lord's righteousness and the bible tells us that in ***(Romans 3:10-19)*** that *there is none righteous apart from Christ.* We are only righteous from what Jesus Christ did. ***(Romans 3:21-26)*** Now I know that it was meant for us to accept God's grace because he already knew that Adam and Eve couldn't obey his commandments by their own strength and Satan wouldn't stop tempting them if Adam and Eve would've rejected the devil so he let them fall anyway because he had already *predestined for us to be conformed into the image of his son amongst many brethren* ***(Romans 8:29)***. Even though I kept my God ordained purpose on hold due to a minor setback by hanging around fools God still had his hand in the situation and caused it to work together for the good of those who love him. ***(Romans 8:28)*** Now does God force you to do anything, no because it wouldn't be a relationship and that's what Calvinist believe in they believe that nothing can stand in the will of God which is true because God is in control of everything but when it comes to your God ordained purpose you have to make a decision to either follow him or make your own choices to whether or not that thing that God showed you is going to come to pass or not so Calvinism is false doctrine. Now in my case I got tired of doing the same thing and being in misery so I decided on May 11, 2014 on Mother's Day to give my life to the Lord. It was my mom's Mother's Day gift and it was also my gift of salvation. I was called out of darkness and into the marvelous light and soon I will elaborate on what it means to be called and what it means to be chosen. I decided that ever since I got saved I will never want to be separated from God ever again. I got baptized on July 6, 2014 so you could have imagined how scared I was to be dipped in water because I couldn't swim (at that time) but after that major event I felt like a new man and I wasn't defined by my past mistakes that I made because I finally understood and came to the realization that the Lord is the only one who I needed to have approval from in my life and not the approval of man. ***(2nd Corinthians 5:17)*** tells us that, *"Therefore if any man be in Christ, he is a new creature, behold old things have passed away and all things are made new."* So, *there is no condemnation for those who are in Christ Jesus who walk not after the flesh but after the spirit.* ***(Romans 8:1)*** Many are called *"Kaleo"* means *"to be invited"* translated in Greek language (the called out are the sinners who accepted salvation and who are translated and invited into the kingdom of God.) but few are chosen. "The chosen" in the Greek means *"eklektos"* which means the elect and the elect are the Christians who bear the fruit of Jesus Christ, whomever is abiding in the spirit when he comes back, and whomever endures till the end for (***Matthew 24:13)*** tells us that *"But he that shall endure unto the end, the same shall be saved."* Jesus

changed my life you'll and if it wasn't for him, I wouldn't be giving you'll my testimony today and the moral of my story is that you can overcome any trial as long as God is on your side. It doesn't matter who counted you out, it doesn't matter who left you, and it doesn't matter what you've been through you are a conquer in Jesus Christ because if he conquered the world then so can you. Jesus isn't saying that you won't go through hardaches and trials and tribulations but he promise's you that nothing shall separate you from the Love of the Lord despite what you're going through, despite what you've been through, and despite what you're going to go through in this life nothing shall separate you from the father. It took me a minute to finally know my true identity in the Lord Jesus Christ but it was worth it and from what I'd experienced with my so called "friends" was worth it because if I haven't gone through that I probably would've been still in sin and I probably would've thought that I was in right standing with the Lord due to my religious beliefs and self-righteousness. In 2012 when they finally builted a church which was once a warehouse where they manufactured items I guess that was the Lord's sovereignty prepping me for obtaining salvation because my grandmother prayed to God to build a church right by her house so she could go to church and not be late.
See how the Lord works he's **omnipotent** (All-powerful), **omniscient** (All-knowing), and **omnipresent** (Everywhere)

CHAPTER TWO

Coming out of churchianity

When people become a Christian in the western part of the world especially in America, they're already programmed to believe that Christianity is churchianity; which is a lie from the pit of hell. I left church for that very reason because I started to grow more intimate with the Lord more outside of church than inside the church. Being a Christian has nothing to do with you attending a building every Sunday even though scripture tells us in ***(Hebrews 10:24-25)*** *"And let us consider how to stimulate one another to love and good deeds, not forsaking our owen assembling together, as is the habit of some, but encouraging one another; and all the more as you see the day drawing near."* It's talking about the remnant of the body of Christ not church buildings because we are the church. The reason why you have many churches now is because they walk after the heathen and follow after their backsliding brothers and sisters in the Lord man-made traditions that they've created. The early church somewhere in time had became defiled and they wanted to be like the Jews having temples and church buildings instead of coming separate like the Lord instructed them to.
This is who started these man-made buildings: **Emperor Constantine** (ca.285-337) In AD 312 Constantine became

Caesar of the western empire and by 324 he became emperor of the entire Roman empire to create church buildings for the cry baby Christians who wanted a temple like the Jews. The original roots of Christian "church buildings," seems to have been little sooner than 320 A.D when Emperor Constantine decided that all of the pagan religions had Temples dedicated to his pagan god *Mithras and other demon gods*, then Constatine decided that the disciples of Jesus Christ, should have Temples also. The archaeologists have found no remains, whatsoever, of anything that could be construed as a Christian religious structure during the lifetimes of Jesus, or of the Twelve, or for 200 years thereafter. This is remarkable in light of the fact that virtually all of the tens of thousands of new converts to Christianity grew up "going to church"—either going to the Jewish Temple or Synagogues, or going to Pagan Temples. It would have been the most logical and natural thing in the world for Christians to build large buildings (as men do today) to have "worship services" in. But they didn't. For two centuries. Why not? Because the concept of "going to Church" on a special day at a special place is totally opposed to the very essence and substance of Jesus and the Church of the Bible that He died to establish. The early church in the book of Acts went from home to home to go preach the gospel not man-made church buildings because the Lord didn't want them to be like the Jews and the pagans who had synagogues and temples to worship pagan gods.

The 1st century early church had homes, out in courtyards, in a long road size (so they didn't have buildings because they were the temple and they disregard pagan practices and synagogues). By the 3rd and 4th century they publicize church and begin to observe and Christianize pagan religious ideas and practices because they wanted to have big churches like the other religions. Church buildings took the place of temples, church in dalmans took the place of temple lands and funds (in other wards 5o1c3 tax building churches that you see around you today, ex: Joel Osteen, T.D Jakes, and other mega church pastors who don't preach unto you the unadulterated gospel of Jesus Christ but a lukewarm gospel etc.) Instead of embracing that under the new covenant with the Holy Spirit dwelling inside of us that we are the temple; they have gone back to old traditions of men and paganistic practices by resurrecting modern-day Jewish Temples and Synagogues of Satan. The reason why the Jews had temples or a building was because of the Judaism law in the old testament but we're not under the law anymore but grace so we are the church. Now do you have to forsake church buildings all together, no just don't make it traditional like you see in most paganistic churches today. Christians come up with the excuse of building churches because in the old testament others in the bible did it (for example, David built a temple in ***Samuel 2:7***) but once again we're not under the law anymore but under grace Jesus already nailed that to the cross; we have God inside of us so manmade buildings aren't necessary. Most of churches today carry on Roman Catholic traditions and rituals that are pagan and an abomination to the Lord. For example the modern day church carried on 3rd century paganistic views like these: (calling their churches temples, participating in having meals in remembrance of the dead after funerals this was created by Roman empire, wearing Roman Catholic robes that came from them Roman empires, having pulpits at the center of the stage, sitting in big tall chairs while deacons are sitting in small chairs, and other Roman paganistic practices and items that are an abomination to the Lord.) Just because you go to church it doesn't mean that you're in right standing with the Lord because you go to church, pay your tithes and offerings, (which it's not for new testament believers from what Paul said in ***Hebrews 7:5*** I'm going to elaborate on tithes and offerings more in this chapter) or just because you're in fellowship with one another just because you profess the same belief. Christians can profess the same belief but they can have two different doctrines and beliefs when it comes to the word of God. For example, one Christian could believe that we're saved by grace through faith in the word of God and another could believe that we should still keep the sabbath and the old laws (which is the old testament laws and sacrifices). That's not agreement or fellowship and I'll continue talking about that in the third chapter of this book but for now let's stay on topic about churchianity. A lot of Christians conduct a traditional religious belief when it comes to being a Christian because that's what we've been indoctrinated with ever since we were little. Just because it sounds and seems like God doesn't mean that it is God and that's the trick with religion, it sounds like God but it isn't. No wonder why the scripture ***(2nd Corinthians 11:14)*** tells us that *Satan transforms himself into an angel of light.* It's true!!! A lot of churches are carrying on traditions of men and tithes and offerings are one example of the traditions of men because it was only meant for the old testament and Jesus redeemed us from the curse of the law because he saw that it wasn't pleasing towards him. Paul said whoever lives by the law will be judged by the law and will be cursed by God and only the righteous will live by faith in the gospel of Jesus Christ. ***(Galatians 3:10-12)*** Paul said that the law (or the old testament laws, including sabbaths and ritualistic animal sacrifices, and tithes and offerings) isn't based on faith but by works and the bible tells us that faith without works is dead ***(James 2:14-26)*** and faith in the gospel is the only thing that'll make you righteous not by your own works trying to obey the ten commandments out of your own strength. You have to have the Holy spirit working in you in order to keep the laws, and you have to have an intimate relationship with God in order to keep the laws. You don't read the bible and try to obey out of your own strength you are to be led by the Holy Spirit and be transformed through your intimacy with God and your relationship with him. This is why Christians can't overcome sin because of self-righteousness and that's why majority of religious Pharisees jump to ***(Matthew 7:1-6, John 8:7, and Romans 3:23)*** when they can't stop sinning in order to come up with an excuse for their sin (completely taking scripture out of context when they do it.) When ***(Romans 6:1-2)*** tells us to refrain from sin. What Paul said in ***Romans 3:23*** *"For all have sinned, and come short of the glory of God."* he was talking about past tense since the fell with Adam and Eve. He wasn't talking present tense because if he was then he would've never mentioned what he mentioned in Romans chapter six about being dead to sin and being made free from sin. The definition of ***have*** means *to experience* and ever since Adam and Eve fell all *have and have* sinned, experience death (spiritually), and none was made righteous outside of Christ ***(Romans 3:10)***. This is when sinful modern-day Christians turn their hearts away from the commandments of God and go on the ways of Balaam or towards a lukewarm gospel that'll make them feel better about their sin. These are the people that the Lord deceives because they don't want to hear, *"Thus said the Lord!!!"* They want to hear someone tell them that it's okay for them to continue in sin. Those are the people that the Lord turns over to a strong delusion because he continued warning them about their sin and he kept telling them to repent but they harden their hearts towards him and this is when the Lord will prophecy falsely to the 'once saved always saved' Christians!!! ***(Ezekiel 14:1-10)*** Lukewarm Christians hate the ten commandments because they hate the Jesus of the bible therefore they want to create their own Jesus which most mega preachers preach today which is the modern-day Jesus and the false grace doctrine which is, “Sin all you want to you’re never going to be perfect.” Which is a flat out lie!!! Let me mind you brethren, the ten commandments were always about love. The first five commandments were for your love for God as being your authority figure and the other five were for your love towards others following up your love for God so if somebody is disobeying those laws especially when it comes to harming others then they never really knew God or loved the Lord with all their heart like the first commandment said. Faith in the gospel is what generates salvation, sanctification, and holiness then the works will follow as your love and intimacy with God increases. The word says, “*faith comes by hearing and hearing by the word of God*” ***(Romans 10:17)***. Jesus knew that it was meant for us to accept his grace because he foresees everything and God doesn’t do plan B’s he always sticks to plan A’s which was for humanity to be transformed into spiritual beings and accept his grace because he knew that we couldn’t keep his commandments out of our own strength. So instead, he took our place on the cross in order to redeem us out of our sin nature so that we can take on the image of him and be transformed into his likeness like we were from the beginning. He didn’t die for us to stay imperfect and sinful beings for ***(Matthew 5:48)*** tells us to *be perfect for even as your father which is in heaven is perfect*. When a lot of “Christians” see that scripture, they think of them obeying the word of God out of their own abilities and when they think like that, they’re taking the scripture out of context because they don’t have the revelation behind that scripture. This is why the Lord led me to entitle the book the way he wanted me to entitle it because what you're reading right now is the *classified revelations from the Father* and what he shares with me on a day to day bases and of course this book isn't really classified because anyone can physically get a hold of this book but only the awaken Christians can receive this revelation because they're not under a religious paradigm anymore so the revelation in the book is still hidden you just have to have a close relationship with the Father to understand it. For those who don't understand this book it's because it's classified and hidden from them due to their sin and for the ones who can interpret this book it's because they're true remnant brothers and sisters in the Lord. So, the identity and revelations of this book is more spiritual than physical because like I said anyone can get their hands on this book the same way anyone can get their hands on the bible and read the bible but the revelation is hidden from them due to their religious paradigms and their sin. Now let's elaborate on the tithes and the offerings!!! A lot of church folk think that tithes and offerings are for the new testament believers as well. This is a lie from hell and I'm going to prove to you how it's a lie from hell. You can read in the book of Deuteronomy and the book of Leviticus on how they did the tithing and the offerings. Tithing was never money it was the produce of the land under the Levitical priesthood, it was the fruit of the land, and the live stocks and it was specifically for the Levitical priesthood because they were a set apart people they weren't considered rich like the Israelites were due to the Israelites prosperity so basically the priesthood was poor and the money that the priesthood were not getting because they had a special service to the Lord in the tabernacle the regular Israelites had a responsibility to pay their taxes and it was never money so that's what their "tithes" were. Now they did have the option to convert their stuff over to money if they wanted to but that was only if the tabernacle or the festival that they had to go to was too far away and they were permitted to convert it to money just in case the things that they were carrying were too heavy and they could do whatever they wanted to do with the money after they converted it to money. Tithing was for the Levitical priesthood, the strangers, and the poor who didn't have income coming in to take care of their family. It was never about money God just wanted people to be taken care of due to the Israelites prosperity from God. Tithing was never for ministers or churches because it's not for the new testament believers. Now that we're under the new covenant Jesus no longer requires us to give a certain amount to the priesthood for example, the ten percent of your money because matter of fact it was more than ten percent it was twenty-three or more percent that you give to the Levitical priesthood and the poor now that we're in the new covenant he just wants us to *freely give* to people like he said in ***(Matthew 10:8)*** because he wants the poor to be taking care of but does your giving have to be limited to money, no. It could be spending time with that person that the Lord has led you to be in fellowship with or cooking and cleaning for the elderly every now and then not everything is about money to people some people just want love and to be showed that somebody actually cares about them. The reason why pastors pick that up from scripture is because it went to the Levitical priesthood so they assume that the same laws in the old testament applies to them or they take ***(2nd Corinthians 9:7)*** out of context when they tell you that Jesus loves a cheerful giver so if you don't give us your money then you're not serving God and that's mixing the holy with the profane; once again it in the old testament the Israelites giving wasn't limited to money and it didn't had to be money if that's the case. So if your pastor is claiming that you're obligated to give them "ten percent" of your income because they're leadership just like the Levitical priesthood use to be to some degree than they should also agree that the money that you gave them should go to the poor and the homeless then and if the money isn't going to the poor and the needy while at the same time the church congregation is still poor while your pastor is driving an expensive car then that should tell you something that "man of God" is a fraud and he will be judged by God on judgement day due to his rebellion. Now the offerings were for the old testament as well to pardon the Israelites from their sins due to animal sacrifices. There were three types of offerings: ***A peace offering, a sin offering***, and ***a burnt offering***. The ***sin offering*** was a sacrifice made according to the Mosaic law which provided atonement for sin. The sin offering was made for sins committed in ignorance or unintentional sins. The ritualistic method of the sin offering and the animal to be offered varied depending on the status of the sinner. For example, a high priest who sinned unintentionally would offer a young bull. A king or a prince would offer a young male goat. People in the private sector would sacrifice a young female goat or lamb unless they were poor in which case they were only required to offer two turtle doves or pigeons. Unlike some other offerings, the sin offering wasn't eaten. The live animal was brought to the alter and the sinner was required to lay his hand on the head of the animal then the animal was killed, at which point that the priest would take some of the blood and put it on the horns altar. Sometimes blood was sprinkled inside the tabernacle. Then all the rest of the blood was poured at the base of the altar. The fat of the sin offer was removed and burned on the alter. But all the rest of the carcass was taken outside the camp to place ceremonially clean where the ashes are thrown and then the carcass was burned in a wood fired on the ash heap. In that way the priest will make an atonement for them for the sin they have committed and they will be forgiven. Let me give you guys some scripture!!! ***(Hebrews 9:22)*** *"In fact the law requires that nearly everything be cleansed with blood and without the shedding of blood there is no forgiveness."* ***Peace offerings*** was a voluntary sacrifice given to God in three ways. First a peace offering could be given as a free will offering meaning that the worshipper was giving the peace offering as a way to say thank you for God's generosity. It's basically a way to praise God for his goodness. The second way a peace offering would be given was alongside a fulfilled vow. An example of this would-be Hannah fulfilled her vow to God by bringing Samuel to the temple and she brought peace offerings with her to express the peace in her heart towards God concerning her sacrifice. The third purpose of peace offerings was to give thanksgiving for God's deliverance and most sacrifices in the old testament were not eaten by worshippers but the peace offering was meant to be eaten. Only a portion of the animal or grain brought to the altar was burned and the rest was given back to the worshipper, the poor, and the hungry so it wasn't just about sacrificing animals to God it's about giving God what he deserves and you keeping the rest to take care of the poor and your family. The third offering was ***burnt offerings*** and a burnt offering is basically the final destruction of the animal (except for the hide) in an effort to renew the relationship between a Holy God and the sinful man. A person could give burnt offerings anytime and it was a sacrifice of general atonement and an acknowledgment of the sin nature and a request for a renewed relationship with God. So when pastors tell you to give up your tithes and offerings they're really saying to you that Jesus didn't pay for all of our sins and he wasn't the full sacrifice for mankind's sin and that's what they believe when they tell you those things when it comes to tithing and offerings because they don't study scripture for themselves and they let the pastor dictate their every move in the church just because of the title that he holds. Being a pastor isn't just a title it's a position that God puts you in to lead God's flock and in order to get that position you have to be ordained and trained by God to be a pastor and even if you are a pastor a degree in pastoring doesn't make you qualified for the job if you haven't gone through the program that every other legit pastor went through which is the testing and the pruning (also known as the wilderness season.) in order for Jesus to walk into his ministry he had to go through the wilderness program to receive it and every other Christian is supposed to go through the same thing if they want to lead God's flock. To chop this thing up with the tithes and offerings you can read Hebrews chapter six through chapter ten, done! Now that we've gotten that covered let's talk about church leadership. Nowadays in these apostate churches they are known to only have one pastor in these buildings nowadays. It's unbiblical to just have one pastor leading God's flock because it's not of the new testament and it considered spiritual suicide if you're a pastor trying to lead God's flock by yourself. If you read the book of Acts when before Jesus had ascended into heaven he didn't just left Peter in charge he left all of the twelve disciples in charge (except for Judas because he died due to his betrayal towards Jesus but they added a new disciple named Matthias when they cast lots between Barsabbas and Matthias.) It's incorrect to just have one pastor running the church and leading God's flock and it's unbiblical to do so. You need multiple apostles in your church congregation to assist you when you're not available to do so and to lead the Lord's sheep and if you look up the nature of a sheep then you would know that sheep are dumb animals and they need a Sheppard to lead them. If you think that you can lead God's flock by yourself as a pastor then you are sadly mistaken and not everyone wants to be taught by the same pastor because some people need other apostles to minister to them based on their spiritual spiritual level; just because you have a church full of Christians doesn't mean that everyone is on the same spiritual level as the other Christian. You need to give other apostles a turn to minster to other people (that's if you're not the only person leading the church and you have multiple apostles in your church.) People want to feel like they're understood and whom they can relate too that's why it's important to have multiple apostles in your church because not everybody can listen to the same person talk about something that they can't relate to and this is why we have people leaving churches because the lack of understanding towards people's situation for the simple fact that you haven't been through what they've been through and then you judge them for that because you don't know how to handle a person whom you can't relate to and if you're not prepared to deal with demonized, hurt, paralyzed, broken, angry, and satanic people then you're not fit for pastorship and this is why you need multiple apostles backing you up and in your church so they can minister to different categories of people in the church. The reason why people leave churches is because the pastors don't have multiple apostles who have different backgrounds and upbringings for that person to relate to them all they have is one pastor in the church who didn't been through what they they've experienced so some people in the church feel that if a pastor can't relate to their story or what they've been through then they're going to leave because nine times out of ten they feel alone and they feel like they're the only one who experienced what they went through and if the pastor haven't been through what a member in that church went through then they're going to judge them for being the way they are and people in the church don't like that so they'll leave. I also feel like if there were more associate pastors in the church then it'll be more effective because each pastor would bring something different to the table for the members of that church to where everybody can be benefited spiritually somehow. Now let's talk about this modern-day gospel that these prosperity preachers are preaching. In this modern-day world Satan has created everything you see in the natural and it's nothing but a counterfeit of God's kingdom in the heavens. Especially when it come to the gospel of Jesus Christ. Everything that you've been taught in church about modern day Christianity is a lie from hell unless you go to an authentic church that teaches the true authentic gospel of Jesus Christ. Nowadays you have preachers who preach unto you a different gospel than what the early church preached. They preached unto you another Jesus or as I would like to call it a Pharisee Jesus or a modern-day Jesus. All of these false apostate churches for example, TD Jakes, Joel Osteen, Joyce Meyer, Creflo Dollar (who just want your dollars), and many prosperity pimps will lead many sheep astray in these last days because they're wolfs in sheep's clothing. Most of them pastors are freemasons and they have people pay them to talk about the prosperity gospel while at the same time not having real revelation from the Lord and talking against sin. You know why because most of these mega churches are nothing but 501c3 government funding behind their churches that's why they can't speak what the Lord tells them because they're in agreement with the state and Satan. You can't drink from the cup of the Lord and the cup of Devils at the same time. Paul said in ***(Galatians 1:8)*** that, *"If any man come preach unto you another gospel let them be accursed."* I'm going to elaborate on this topic a little bit more!!! The problem with these Modern-day churches is that they don't preach the true authentic unadulterated gospel of Jesus Christ; now don't get me wrong there's nothing wrong with teaching about prosperity but it's how you teach it. You won't get God's promises first of all without going through a season of trying and testing and that's biblical from what I've read. (1 Timothy 3:1-13) In order for Jesus to die for our sins and walk towards the promise land he had to yield to the wilderness season to be proven so he could walk into the promise land. Satan tempted Jesus in Luke chapter four with all of the things that the God was going to give him pun intended he was God in the flesh he just had a different name and his name was called Jesus. So, if you didn't go through the trial and tribulations that were required in order to become a pastor then you're operating in a counterfeit spirit because a true prophet would've been humbled before they could obtain that ministry because they've already been proven and tried. I don't care if you got a degree in order to preach to people you have to go through the same program that Jesus went through. Another famous lie that pastors spread is that Jesus did away with the Law (The Torah Old testament), well the question is what laws did Jesus did away with and which ones he didn't do away with we're going to break that down as we go deeper into the things of God but first we're going to go over the basis of what the Law really is. When most Christians say that Jesus did away with the Law they're referring to the Old testament (Torah/Law of Moses which is the Law of God but it was given to Moses) which isn't true according to ***(Matthew 5:17-19)*** [17] *"Do not think that I have come to abolish the* ***Law [Torah]*** *or the Prophets; I have not come to abolish them but to fulfill them.* [18] *For truly, I say to you, until heaven and earth pass away, not an iota, not a dot, will pass from the Law until all is accomplished.* [19] *Therefore whoever relaxes one of the least of these commandments and teaches others to do the same will be called least in the kingdom of heaven, but whoever does them and teaches them will be called great in the kingdom of heaven."* Jesus told us to keep the Torah because He kept the Torah (Old testament) because Jesus was a Jew and he came from Hebrew roots, also Jesus is the Word according to ***(John 1:1-3 & John 1:14)*** Jesus is the second piece to the trinity; He's also the son of God because he came from GOD not only making Him God in the flesh because he came from God but Jesus must submit to GOD'S will because Jesus is the Word and if the Word (which is Jesus) doesn't submit to the Father then somethings wrong. The Famous scriptures that a lot of Christians like to take out of context to justify their modern-day Christianity or religious traditions today are ***(Acts 15:6-11, Galatians 3:10-14, Galatians 4:8-10, Colossians 2:16-17)*** *"So therefore Jesus did away with the Law."* (Lawless Christians speaking lol) First off if Jesus did away with those things then that would make him a lawless Messiah which would make him sinful therefore it would make him qualified to not die for our sins because He'd be just like us who were sinners. When Paul speaks of "Under the law" He's talking about the curse of the law. Sin is lawlessness!!! When Adam and Eve sinned, they became under the law meaning to be governed by God's laws because of their transgression in the garden of Eden. Go rob a store and see if the judge doesn't judge you according to their laws in the state that you stay in, they'll do just that it's the same with God. The curse of the law isn't the law of God the curse of the law is you breaking the law due to lawlessness and you transgressing the Torah (Law of God/Old testament) and the curses come upon you as a result of you not keeping God's statues and commandments. The Christians that think that the Law is burdensome should read ***(Psalms 119:105)*** that scripture is in reference to David keeping the Torah (Old testament) and the Torah (Old testament) was a lamp unto David's feet and a light unto

David's path even the Old testament says that the Torah isn't burdensome according to ***(Deuteronomy 30:11)*** Christians who still think that Jesus did away with the Law should really examine the New Testament Paul didn't teach from the New Testament Paul taught from the Torah because every Saturday they would have teachings in the Jewish synagogues every Sabbath day reading the scrolls. The Torah wasn't just for the Jews it was for the Gentiles who were practitioners in pagan practices and origins who came into believing in the messiah. The Torah which is God's law is for everyone to keep. Once you come into faith by believing in the messiah you become a spiritual Jew according to ***(Romans 2:29)*** and you are to keep the Torah. If believers were still gentiles when they get saved (Gentile-pagan practicers) then they wouldn't be believers because they're still transgressors of the Law. As believers in Jesus we are to keep the *Mosheh* (which is the Law of Moses in Hebrew). Now we are going to get into what laws did Jesus do away with. So now that we have a clear understanding that Jesus didn't came to do away with the (Torah/ Old testament) well the question is what laws did he do away with then? Jesus did away with the Oral Torah (which was the traditions of the elders) ***Acts 15:10*** is talking about the oral torah that the people who came into the Christian faith had to keep in order to become disciples and that was physical circumcision for and the traditions of the elders ***(Mark 7:5-9)*** is a perfect example of this. It's not the scripture (Torah) or the Old testament it's the tradition of the elders that was a burden to the people. An example of the traditions of the elders today would be church people or religious folk that throw away the Old testament in order to celebrate their pagan holidays and Christianize false god worship like ***Christmas*** (worships false god Zeus, or Nimrod when Jeremiah 10 speaks against it etc.) ***Easter*** (Eostre or Ostara, the ancient Germanic goddess of spring) ***Valentine's day*** (Celebration to the false god Lupercalia) the same thing Christians are doing today are doing the same thing that the Israelites did in the Old testament another example would be when Ezekiel was shown in the temples what the Israelites were doing in the temples and how they were defiling the temples (having a form a godliness but were really worshipping false gods like weeping for Tamuz for example). We Christians aren't to supposed to be celebrating holidays we are to celebrate Holydays because that's our covenant being spiritual Israel. Here are a list of feast days or Holy days we can keep a Christians being spiritual Israel of the new covenant:

Holydays for believers

Feast of Trumpets: September 10-11 ***(Celebrate coming together with the saints, celebrate being directed by God, Blowing the trumpets, it's a Holy convocation day i.e. prepare food beforehand, no work, no ungodly video games, and have a feast.)***

Day of Atonement aka Celebrating the desperate need for Yahweh: September 19-20

- ***We learn that when Christ returns, satan will be put away for a while and we will finally be at one with God without the devil causing trouble lol.***
- ***Atonement king of means "at-one-ment" On this day God tells us to fast for 24 hours from sundown to sundown. This teaches us that if we do not become at one with God, we have no hope and will die.***

1. ***Do a 24hr fast***
2. ***Humbly seek God***
3. ***Holy Convocation day no servile work, no ungodly video games.***

Feast of Tabernacles: September 24th- October 1st
The main purpose is celebrating the upcoming 1000-year reign of Christ, celebrating how the Lords dwell with His people, celebrating how God will rebuild the earth.

1. ***Imagine God's kingdom here on earth***
2. ***Discuss how things will be different when Christ comes.***
3. ***Have a feast***
4. ***Holy convocation: Ye shall do no work***

The last day: Sundown October 1st- October 2 the main purpose in celebrating this Holyday is the upcoming end of suffering and peace on earth.

1. ***Celebrating the ultimate culmination of God's plan there's resurrection of the dead from hell to attend the judgement and the judgment of the vast majority of all human beings who ever lived.***
2. ***Celebrating the upcoming new heaven, new earth and new Jerusalem.***

- ***Assemble everyone together to discuss what the culmination of God's plan means to you.***
- ***No work***
- ***Have a feast***

Passover: March 31st-April 1st The Passover is a time to remember God's angel passing over the houses of His people, sparing the firstborn sons of Egypt. Celebrate Christ's death on Passover.

1. ***Sinners cannot celebrate Passover you must be sin free Exodus 12:43-47***
2. ***Take Communion in remembrance of Christ death for our sins (1st Corinthians 11:24-25)***
3. ***Watch a movie about Jesus's death***
4. ***Passover meal should be eaten in one home not home to home (Exodus 12:43-47)***
5. ***It's a Holy convocation day and no servile work***
6. ***Have a feast!!!***

Feast of unleavened Bread: April 1-8 the main purpose of this Holyday is to live a sinless life of the Lord, celebrate Jesus's death here are some examples of unleavened bread:

- ***Cracked rye bread***
- ***Unleavened Bread***
- ***Tortilla***
- ***Danish rye bread***
- ***Indian naan bread***
- ***Pita Bread***
- ***Indian Chapati Bread***

How to celebrate unleavened bread

1. ***Do baptisms***

   1.5 Remove all leaven from your home on the 1st day of the feast as an example of removing sin Exodus 12:15

2. ***Eat unleavened bread daily to represent a sin free life. Note: Leaven is a symbol for sin unleavened bread has no yeast to puff it up, so it is flat. We also learn that the next step in God's plan is to try to take the sin out of our lives. Sin is like leavening, it puffs up and makes us proud. God wants us humble, like the flat bread.***
3. ***Take Communion daily in remembrance of Christ for our sins.***

Feast of first fruits: April 7th-8th The purpose of this Holyday is the resurrection of Christ from the dead a celebration of being thankful to God for providing for you and your family. Celebrating Jesus's resurrection from the dead; as now we ascend into heaven with the Father. Paul tells us explicitly that Christ is the first fruits of those who will be raised from the dead. ***(1st Corinthians 15:20-23)***

How to celebrate first fruits feasts

1. *Worshipping and Thanking God for providing for you.*
2. *Worshipping and Thanking God for Jesus resurrection*
3. *Have a feast*
4. *Watch a movie about Jesus*
5. *Holy Convocation*

Counting the Omer: Sundown April 7th-26th The purpose of this Holyday is anticipating the engulfing of the Holy Spirit celebrating the Israelites exodus from Egypt till the day the law (Torah) was given to Moses. It is the Jewish tradition that it took 50 days to walk from Egypt to Mount Sinai where the law was given to Moses Celebrating Jesus's death as a sacrifice for our sins till the day of Pentecost when the Holy Spirit was given.

1. ***The counting of the omer is done 50 days in a room from sundown day after the Passover sabbath day, until the sundown day of starting of the feast weeks.***

For instance, if April 7th 2019 is the day after the Passover, sabbath day you would say something like, "Thank God for the blood of the lamb that allowed for the Israelite Children to be spared in Egypt and led to their exodus from Egypt. Thank you, Yahweh, for the blood of the lamb of God Jesus that allows for our sins to be blotted out. Thank you for your laws and the gift of your Holy Spirit. Today is the First day of the counting of the omer."

2. ***On the 50th day you declare that day a Holy convocation to you see day of Pentecost.***
3. ***Being grateful in your heart and looking forward to the next celebration of God's goodness.***

The day of Pentecost: Sundown May 26th-27th The purpose of this Holyday is celebrating the giving of the Holy Spirit.

1. ***Celebrating the coming down of the Law***
2. ***Celebrating the coming down of the Holy Spirit.***

- ***Everyone should be in one accord; in one place; and seeking the Holy Spirit.***
- ***Celebrating having the Holy Spirit in you.***
- ***You are not supposed to work***
- ***It is a Holyday so everything you should be doing should be based on God.***
- ***Have a feast***
- ***Do baptisms.***

Now let's go over Acts 15:10 in the proper context! What ***Acts 15:10*** is referring to is the traditions of the Pharisees and the scribes according to ***Matthew 23:1***. ***Matthew 23:1*** was talking about how the Pharisees were supposed to be teaching the law of Moses or the Law of God (Torah) in the synagogues but the Pharisees were keeping their own traditions and not the Torah and the Pharisees started to bind them with heavy burdens hard to bear and lay them on men's shoulders again the same example of this would be a reference to ***Mark 7:5-9*** the Pharisees didn't even obey their own manmade traditions but wanted to be in the synagogue and be called rabbi when Jesus said call no man rabbi except the Father. Now let's get into if the Lord wants us to keep the Sabbath. Again, the Sabbath (known as the ***shabbat***) is a part of the Ten commandments and The Lord didn't do away with them because he told us to keep them for generations to generations according to ***(Exodus 31:16)***. In Matthew Jesus didn't violate the sabbath by healing people on the sabbath and stuff like that Jesus had to redo the traditions of the Pharisees and the Scribes because they would loosen their ox's or donkeys to go and give it water when they were supposed to rest so it was them doing evil on the sabbath day so when it came down to Jesus his followers asked Him is it lawful to heal on the sabbath and Jesus responded to them *""If any of you has a sheep and it falls into a pit on the Sabbath, will you not take hold of it and lift it out? How much more valuable is a person than a sheep! Therefore, it is lawful to do good on the Sabbath."* Then he said to the man, *"Stretch out your hand." So, he stretched it out and it was completely restored, just as sound as the other.* A lot of Christians also light to take ***(Matthew 11:28-30)*** out of context because ***(Matthew 11:28-30)*** isn't a scapegoat for you to not keep the Sabbath it's telling torah examiners to dump the traditions of the scribes and Pharisees and take up the Lord's yoke and he will give you rest because His yoke is easy and His burden is light (basically Jesus was implying that if you keep the Torah the way you're supposed to as He keeps the Torah then you're burden will be lighter than you trying to follow the traditions of the Pharisees and scribes who don't keep the Torah but their own traditions etc.) Now see how the Old testament is agreeing with the New Testament, The Old testament says*, "For this commandment that I command you today is not too hard for you, neither is it far off."* ***(Deuteronomy 30:11) and*** Jesus says *"My yoke is easy and my burdens are light"* ***(Matthew 11:28-30)*** The two compliments each other because the Lord is One, he doesn't contradict Himself. The Law which is the Torah isn't bad it's good and Holy ***(Romans 7:12)*** For the law of the Spirit of life in Christ Jesus had made me free from the law of sin and death [consequences of breaking the Torah] For what the law couldn't do in that it was weak through the flesh (meaning that they couldn't obtain righteousness through obeying out of their own strength) God did by sending His own son in the likeness of sinful flesh that ***the righteousness requirement of the Law*** might be fulfilled in us who don't walk according to the flesh but according to the

Holy Spirit. ***(Romans 10:3)*** is the example of religious folk following their own way telling you that the Torah is done away with and they establish their own righteousness like the Pharisees and Scribes [doing right in their own eyes and have not submitted to the Torah or the Law of God] for Christ is the end of the law for righteousness to everyone who believes (Romans 10:4) meaning state of completion or the end goal because Jesus kept the Law of God (Torah). Christ is the end of the Law not it's abolition of the Torah that is God statues and commandments. Now if you have a false doctrine that teaches otherwise that you don't have to keep the Sabbath because Jesus did away with it then you're under a false doctrine and a false grace because God's grace isn't a license for sin it's an supernatural work that's being doing through you by you being empowered by the Holy Spirit in order to keep God's laws and His commandments Jesus said if you love Him keep His commandments. The ***Dietary laws*** are still in effect because whatever God calls an abomination is an abomination and that will never change just read Leviticus 11 for the examples of what foods to eat and what foods not to eat. Now I'm going to give you some points on how to discern if your pastor is in error when it comes to the word of God and what to do if you're in that situation:

- ***Any pastor who's still struggling with sin especially sexual sin and who isn't preaching against sin is a false pastor and isn't ordained by God to preach and I would remove myself from that church.***

- ***Any church congregation that only has one pastor needs to have more than just one teaching God's sheep because in the book of Acts the twelve disciples would be teaching multiple people about the gospel. It wasn't just Peter and the rest of the disciples stayed hidden in the background, it was all of them teaching each other what Jesus had taught them before he ascended into heaven. You need multiple apostles to teach and to grow God's flock!!! A lot of pastors think that they don't need multiple apostles to teach God's flock but it's necessary because what if something happens to the main leader in the church, somebody needs to back him up. Now am I saying leave the church, it depends on the pastor. I recommend you seeking the Holy spirit and if He's leading you to share this video you can share it with your pastor.***

- ***Any pastor who's in adultery, gay, or has a women pastoring doesn't know God and I would leave that church immediately especially if it's a woman pastoring and if that's the case, she's operating in a Jezebel spirit and I would leave that church.***

Now I'm going to demonstrate to you how to discern between the false Jesus that these prosperity false preachers are teaching and the real authentic Jesus which is of the bible:

The False Jesus Christ

- **Born as a man who was promoted to deity**
- **Never says anything negative**
- **Doesn't have multiple apostles in the church to lead God's flock**
- **Disregards repentance of sins**
- **Rejects the Holy Spirit and the power and gifts of the Holy Spirit (2 Timothy 3:5)**
- **Gives health, wealth, and happy feelings**
- **Doesn't convicts people of sins and doesn't preach against sin**
- **Gives suggestions instead of commandments**
- **Doesn't tell you the truth and loves to sugarcoat and twist scripture to satisfy your lust.**
- **Serves your will; instead of you submitting to God's will for your life. ("Do what thou wilt!!!" Alesister Crowley)**
- **Exalts signs, wonders, and mysticism above God's word.**
- **Encourages you to love yourself and gratify your fleshly desires**
- **Believes in once saved always saved**
- **Tells you to do away with the Law (Torah) promotes lawlessness, you can celebrate pagan holidays and traditions, you can eat whatever you want, come as you are standoff never transformed to Holiness and goes against the Father's instruction to create a new religion that goes against the Old testament.**

The Real Jesus Christ

- **Born as God Almighty in the flesh**
- **Warns of sin, judgement, and hell**
- **Does have multiple apostles in the church to lead God's flock**
- **Commands repentance of sins**
- **Accepts the Holy Spirit and the power and gifts of the Holy Spirit (1st Corinthians 12:3-12 and John 14:26)**
- **Gives you salvation, hope, peace, love, and joy**
- **Hates sin and exposes the truth about sin**
- **Commands with divine authority**
- **Offends the world with truth**
- **You serve and submit to his will for your life not the other way around (1 Corinthians 6:19-20 and Romans 12:1)**
- **Warns of false signs, wonders, magnifies God's word**
- **Demands that emotion, experience, and opinion conform to sound doctrine**
- **Encourages you to deny yourself**
- **Your salvation is conditional and 'once saved always saved' is a lie from hell (Matthew 24:13 and John 15:2-6)**
- **Fulfilled the Law of Moses, Prophets and Psalms Tells you to keep the Torah the old and new testament goes together because the LORD is One. Commands Holiness and separation from pagan holidays and pagan clothes like makeup, hair weave, jewelry and you can't eat what you want because you're under dietary laws.**

> This is how you can discern between the false Jesus and the real Jesus Christ which is of the bible and nowadays people hate the truth and they hate the Jesus of the bible so what they'll do is twist scripture and try to make it fit their fleshly desires and carnal sin nature because they despise the truth.

In the bible, it talks about in the last days there will be people who will despise the truth, and leave the faith to go after doctrines of devils and demons. ***(1ST Timothy 4:1)*** *Now the Spirit speaketh expressly, that in the latter times some shall depart from the faith, giving heed to seducing spirits, and doctrines of devils.* The false Jesus was created by mankind and doctrines of demons because they receive not the truth so the Lord turned them over to their lust and to their deception all because they've failed to receive truth from the Lord. They don't want to hear, *"Thus said the Lord thy God!!!"* They want to hear a word from a prophet that's going to tell them what they want to hear instead of what they need to hear; and because of the idolatry that's in their harden hearts the Lord will prophecy falsely to them especially when God has told them no about a particular thing and they still want to go ahead and pursue that thing that the Lord told them no about. Let's go through scripture!!! ***(Ezekiel 14:1-11)*** *Then came certain of the elders of Israel unto me, and sat before me. 2And the word of the Lord came unto me, saying, 3 Son of man, these men have set up their idols in their heart, and put up the stumbling block of their iniquity before their face: should I be enquired*

of at all by them? 4 *Therefore speak unto them, and say unto*
them, Thus saith the Lord God; Every man of the house of
Israel that setteth up his idols in his heart, and putteth the
stumbling block of his iniquity before his face, and cometh
according to the multitude of his idols;
5 *That I make take the house of Israel in their own heart,*
because they are all estranged from me through their idols.
6 *Therefore say unto the house of Israel, Thus saith the Lord*
God; Repent and turn yourselves from your idols; and turn
away your faces from all your abominations. 7 *For everyone*
of the house of Israel, or of the stranger that sojourneth in
Israel, which separateth himself from me, and setteth up his
idols in his heart, and putteth the stumblingblock of his
iniquity before his face, and cometh to a prophet to enquire
of him concerning me; I the Lord will answer him by myself:
8 *And I will set my face against that man, and will make him*
a sign and a proverb, and I will cut him off from the midst of
my people; and ye shall know that I am the Lord. 9 *And if the*
prophet be deceived when he hath spoken a thing, I the Lord
have deceived that prophet, and I will stretch out my hand
upon him, and will destroy him from the midst of my people
Israel. 10 *And they shall bear the punishment of their*
iniquity: the punishment of the prophet shall be even as the
punishment of him that seeketh unto him; 11 *That the house of*
Israel may go no more astray from me, neither be polluted
anymore with all their transgressions; but that they may be
my people, and I may be their God, saith the Lord God. God
is the chief and commander and whatever he says to you

goes no matter if we like it or not and if you keep on trying to ask God after he gave you a warning then he'll allow you to be deceived due to the idolatry that's in your heart knowing that he told you no about a certain thing. The same thing had happened to me once.

CHAPTER THREE

Fellowship & agreement

A lot of christains think that fellowhip is just you hanging out with another Christian just because you'll profess the same belief and that's not true and there's so much false doctrine in the body of Christ when it comes to fellowshipping with another believer that Christians just throw the word "fellowship" around like it's nothing. Let me remind you, fellowship is you being in harmony with another believer meaning that you're in agreement with each other. This means that the both of you are likeminded and are on one accord like I said in chapter two. You can't have one believer who believes that we're saved by grace through faith in the gospel and the other believes that we're saved by works righteousness, that's not agreement that's confusion. Christians assume that they're this big threat towards the enemy because they have the Holy Spirit and a lot of these spiritual gifts when the enemy can see in the spiritual realm that they're not in agreement with each other. A lot of believers take ***(Matthew 18:20)*** out of context because they're reading it from a carnal lense regarding the numbers of saints gathered in the Lord's name yes, it's true that if two or more are gathered in his name then he's in the midst but you guys could have two completely different doctrines and denominations being Christians that the enemy can see in the spiritual realm and he can mess that up if you guys aren't on one accord and in agreement with each other. For example, in David's Elles book called *Sovereign God* there was a chapter in his book where he talked about three different Christians prayed to God three different prayers regarding one person's life before that person died. One Christian prayed if it was God's will to take him then let it be done, the second Christian prayed to the Lord for the Lord to heal him, and the third Christian prayed to the Lord to take him. Now let me ask you this, is that being in agreement? NO! Afterwards the Lord took that patient home because there wasn't really any agreement going on between the three Christians. You have to be on one accord as well in order for God to move how you want him to move; otherwise he'll choose his will by default. Paul talks about being on one accord in scripture. ***(Philippians 2:1-2)*** *So if there is any encouragement in Christ, any comfort from love, any participation in spirit, any affection and sympathy, complete my joy by being of the same mind, having the same love, being in full accord and one mind.* Let me tell you guys a story about what happened to me a while ago. Back in 2015 (and this was right after I graduated) way back in December I remember praying to God about sending me someone whom I could fellowship with because I was bored and I got tired of sitting around in the house; and at the time I didn't know what fellowship really was so at the time I assumed that fellowship mean just hanging out with another Christian just because you'll believe in Jesus.

No that's not the case at all!!! The question is do you'll believe in the true Jesus? Remember in the second chapter where I gave you guys bullets on how to discern between a false Jesus and the true authentic Jesus, well in this case the both of us weren't really in agreement and I thought that we were in agreement just because we went to church, and we profess that we believed in Jesus Christ. Let me tell you guys something, just because you go to church don't mean that you're in right standing with the Lord and yes, I know that the word does tells us to ***not forsake the assembly*** in ***(Hebrews 10:25)*** but at the same time you're not going to be judged based on the fellowship that you had with your brothers and sisters in the Lord; you're going to be judged by your fellowship with the Lord and the work that you did as a Christian while you were on this earth. Religious folk take that scripture out of context because they want to find a reason for people to keep going to these apostate "once saved always saved and false doctrine churches." I'm not saying that it's bad to go church if they're preaching the true authentic gospel of Jesus Christ nor am I saying that it's bad to fellowship with other believers but you guys have to be in agreement in order to have fellowship with one another. The Lord isn't bound to church just like he isn't bound to the letter (which is the word of God) because we're not under the law anymore but the grace of God so as long as something is quickened by the Holy spirit then you can listen to it. For example, God may use secular music to encourage you with something but it has to be quickened by the Holy spirit even though secular music is bad and believers shouldn't be listening to secular music God can use almost anything to encourage you so they're both paradoxes. Once again, we're not bound to the law anymore! People come up and continue with their manmade traditions and stamp God on it because they want to put God in a box when *his thoughts are higher than our thoughts and his ways aren't our ways.* ***(Isaiah 55:8)*** God isn't bound to church because he's ***omni-present*** *(meaning Everywhere)* nor is he bound to manmade religion because he's ***omni-potent*** (*meaning all-powerful)* so he can do whatever he wants to do because he's GOD so give him the freedom and the liberty of being GOD. The Lord didn't make religion, men made religion because they wanted to take credit of the gospel that Jesus preached and they wanted to take credit for their own gospel that they created in their mind when our thinking without the Holy spirit is flawed. That is what the bible means when it says to *not lean unto your own understanding*! ***(Proverbs 3:5)*** Yes, I know that *in the beginning was the word, and the word was with God, and the word was God* ***(John 1:1)*** but he isn't bound to the letter like we think he is. I'm going to give you guys another example, some Christians think that Jesus can't manifest himself to people anymore because they believe that he won't reveal himself until the second coming, that's not true either. Once again God isn't in a box! When you have a Christian who's religious, you'll are not in agreement. I remember watching Christian testimonies on YouTube where people had a personal and fleshly encounter with the

Lord face to face still today so he isn't bound to the letter or law. Now I want to go into more detail about the "fellowship" that me and a friend of mine had in late December of 2015. Remember when I told you guys that I prayed to the Lord about sending me somebody to fellowship with because I was bored, well it happened. During that time, I was in church and I was currently going to church when we first met for the first time after his early departing from high school during his freshman year and at the time my junior year because he suffered from social anxiety and the school wasn't really the best environment for him. His name is William After bible study one Wednesday evening sometime around the month of June during summer time in 2015 we bumped into each other walking out of the church and we chopped it up with each other right then and there. During our reconciliation, he basically recommended that we should hang out with each other because we didn't see each other in a long time so I'd agreed and we decided to exchange numbers with each other and then we parted ways. I didn't hear from him since!!! Six months later prior to us seeing each other for the first time in June out of the blue William decided to call me out of nowhere on a Wednesday night of bible study when I couldn't find a ride to bible study. I answered the phone, while on the phone he asked me if I had a ride to go to bible study that night and I told him no. So, he offered me a ride to go to bible study because I told him I didn't have a ride that night and he told me that he was going to pick me up from my house by 5:30 p.m. sharp. Bible study starts around 6:30 p.m. and he didn't pull up to my house till around 6:15 despite what he told me when we were on the phone about him coming to my house around 5:30. When William pulled up in the drive way I got in the car and we drove off to bible study. During the drive, he stopped at the first red light coming from my neighborhood and heading towards the main road on the way to church. During the red light, he turned on the light inside the car and he said to me, "Yo X I have to tell you something me and my father got into an altercation and he scratched me on the face when we fought." I responded, "Why were you guys fighting for?" He told me, "It's because he's a narcissist!" I responded, "That's messed up man is he abusive too?" William replied, "Yes he is abusive and he favors Jasmine (his sister) over me because I'm autistic and she's not." Astonished from what William was telling me I responded, "I know how you feel bro I've been in your shoes because my dad was also abusive and I was also autistic due to my mother having a birth defect." During the ride on the way to church I confided in William about my past to instill Godly counsel and confidence inside of him. After church, he dropped me off to my house and left to go home. During the rest of our conciliation we had fun, we went skating, and last year of May 2016 we had went to one of his friend's graduation cookout and I had the best time of my life. At that time, I was still dealing with the residue of the spirit of rejection and the Lord used him for a season to heal me from my wounds even though we were dealing with similar experiences and issues. He taught me that it didn't matter what the outsiders think or say as long as you're comfortable in who you are in Christ then that's all that matters. The downfall of hanging out with him is that when we would hang out with each other along with my classmates that I was friends with during the beginning of my freshman school year in college that he would act worldly, play a lot of secular music when we would go places with my colleagues, smoke a lot of cigars, and cuss a lot and I've noticed that every time we got around my colleagues he switches up and start acting worldly. The world would look at that and call it a diagnosis of schizophrenia but I knew that it was another characteristic of the spirit of rejection because the spirit of rejection fears being themselves in front of people so what that person will do is create a false image of who they really are to cover up the flaws and insecurities that they have creating an alter ego or personality for themselves in order to be accepted and liked by other people. Despite his flaws we had good times together and he was a great friend that the Lord used to encourage me to cope with my social anxiety until he exposed his heart towards me and gave me red flags.

One day me and William decided to hang out on a hot Saturday to go get some Dano's pizza, he would pick me up as usual and we would go somewhere just to get out of the house and have fun. On our way to Dano's pizza I've felt a heaviness come upon me like I cannot describe it was probably my spiritual discernment at the time but during the time that I felt that heaviness come upon me like that while we were in the company of each other was probably a red flag from God convicting me of something. It was probably the fact that he didn't want me in company with William anymore for the simple fact that he did tell me that it was a seasonal friendship and the friendship probably expired not me having any notice of the transition and change of the season during the "fellowship" that I had with William. I couldn't stand listening to secular music with him in the car because unlike him I understood what it really meant to be a disciple in Christ and what Christianity really intel's on so I took my walk with the Lord seriously on the other hand; William probably knew God from a church perspective and an religious perspective but he doesn't know God from a relationship perspective and he doesn't know the authentic Gospel of Jesus Christ he probably believed in the false grace doctrine which is "once saved always saved." You could discern it by the lift style that another Christian is living and how to discern it is that you line it up with scripture and follow your convictions. What does scripture say about it?! ***(1st Corinthians 5:11)*** *But now I have written unto you not to keep company, if any man that is called a brother be a fornicator, or covetous, or an idolator, or a railer, or a drunkard, or an extortioner; with such a one no not to eat.* If that's the case then me and William were never in agreement from the beginning because we had two completely different doctrines and two completely different Jesus's. My doctrine was the true authentic gospel; his doctrine was a counterfeit "once saved always saved" doctrine. My Jesus is the Jesus of the bible and the one who was despised by the world because of his calling; his Jesus was a man-made Jesus that the world loves and accepts because it's traditions of men all because those "Christians" don't like to receive conviction and truth so as a result they harden their hearts, disregard the word of God, create their own Jesus and what they feel like Jesus should be like when Jesus never changes and its scripture. ***(Hebrews 13:8)*** This is how different denominations get started because of different beliefs, offenses, and not staying on one accord like Paul recommended in 1st Corinthians. Once again God the creator of the universe didn't make religion; manmade religion and it's cause division in the body of Christ and the bible says that there's no division in Christ and he's not the author of confusion either so why is it that we still have denominations today? God can still use it and turn it around for his good and for his purpose which means that he's using the denominational church to test his true saints to see if they truly know him or not. This is one of God's strategies to separate the wheat from the tares and to test those who really belong to him (which is the true body of Christ and not man-made buildings.) Anyways, when I was continuing being in "fellowship" with this "brother" in the Lord I felt like our relationship was ending and the Lord was showing me that through conviction of the Holy Spirit. In my friends presence I felt a lot of guilt and agony because we hand a lot in common relatively but not so much spiritually and conviction of the Holy Spirit is bigger than your personal feelings and what you want and desire for yourself because you've been brought with a price just like ***(1st Corinthians 6:20)*** says that you are so really it's not about you anymore; it's about God giving you his Holy Spirit so that he can work through you as long as you're surrendering to his Spirit so that he can manifest his kingdom in the earth realm and save souls. Me and my friend weren't in agreement because we had two completely different doctrines so therefore, we weren't in fellowship despite what churchianity tells you what "fellowship" is. You are only in fellowship with another believer when you're in agreement with each other (meaning being on one accord doctrine wise, spiritual wise, and walking on the same path which is the narrow path.) If your brother or sister in the Lord don't meet those requirements then you're not in fellowship with one another because you're not on one accord with each other doctrinally, spiritually, and you're on a different path then that other Christian whom you claim to be in fellowship with. You're not in fellowship with another believer if you're in the Holy Spirit submitting to God's will and his leading for your life while on the other hand your brother or sister in the Lord are pursuing their own will (self-will), not yielding to the Holy Spirit, not spending time with God, and just operating under an anti-christ spirit are not, so you guys aren't in fellowship with each other. Well you might ask me how is it that pursuing your own will as a Christian got anything to do with you being in fellowship with another believer, I'll explain to you what I mean. For example, we already know that we've been brought with a price as believers because ***(1stCorinthains 6:20)*** tells us that so it's common sense that we are to seek God's will in every situation for ***(Matthew 6:33)*** tells us to *seek ye first the kingdom of God, and his righteousness; and all these things shall be added unto you.* If you see another believer not doing that then they're not in God's will for their lives and they're operating under an anti-christ spirit because nowadays Christians develop this worldly mentality where they believe that whatever career path that they choose to do is God's will for their lives (that is not only false doctrine but you're operating under occultic beliefs as well.) I'll explain to you how!!! For example, an old English occultist named Aleister Crowley came up with this satanic philosophy that men are gods and they can do whatever they want to do thinking that their personal choices are better than the Lord's plan for their lives. That isn't the first satanist who believe that men are to be gods like GOD himself; Satan himself also believes it because of pride according to ***(Genesis 3:5)*** where he tempted Eve to eat the forbidden fruit. Not only did he tempt her to eat the forbidden fruit he told her an lie and tried to convince her that if she at the forbidden fruit that she could be like God herself knowing good and evil (that theology out of the three sin triggers my friend is known as *the pride of life* the other two are: *the lust of the flesh* and the *lust of the eye*) This satanic philosophy is best known as the phrase ***'Do what thou wilt'*** (in other wards be your own god do what you want to do, your personal goals are better than

God's plans due to the amount of money or the level of fame you'll get pursuing this career and don't worry about doing God's will for your life because you're an god because you came from him yourself) that isn't true! Yes, you came from God and you were created by him but that doesn't mean that you're like God himself. We've fallen from God's grace because of Adam and Eve and he redeem us out of our sin nature by the ultimate sacrifice of Jesus Christ so we are to be transformed and perfected into the image of his son like he intended for it to be ***(Romans 8:29)*** tells us this. It was meant for the fall to happen and it was meant for us to need a savior because he foreknew and saw that our first parents were going to fall anyway because satan probably wouldn't probably stopped tempting them even if they were to walk away from the first temptation so God allowed them to fall. Now am I saying that God couldn't stop the whole situation from happening if he wants to, no because he's God he can do what he wants it's just wasn't his will for us to be that way. His will was for us to conform to the image of his son Jesus Christ. He foreknew everything because he knows *the beginning to the end* ***(Isaiah 46:10)*** so the Lord is sovereign. Bible prophecy is being played out right before our very eyes so that's just goes to show that he isn't a liar nor is he the son of man that he shall repent. Even when knowing that what makes you think that the Lord doesn't have your plan for your life already figured out by now because he's ten steps ahead of you and *his ways are past finding out* ***(Romans 11:33)***. Another false doctrine is Calvinism!!!

Calvinist believe that no matter what happens nothing can stand in the way of the will of God, that is true but it's not truth. Yes, it may be true that nothing can stand in the way of the will of God (his general will; which is to get souls saved and to manifest his kingdom in the earth realm) but some of his promises are conditional when his promises require your will as well and what I mean by your will I'm talking about you doing your part in the promise that God made to you: (Whether it's an God ordained spouse, your salvation, God's purpose and destiny for your life, having children etc.) Some religious folk will tell you that if it's God's will it shall come to pass because *the Lord's word doesn't return unto him void* ***(Isaiah 55:11)*** but once again that may be true but it's not truth. If you don't have faith and you're not doing your part in what the Lord told you to do then it will not come to pass and you can see that with Solomon he wrecked God's promise for him in ***(1st Kings 11: 1-13)***. It doesn't matter, your will and faith are required in order to bring that promise to pass. Another example, God's promises are unconditional when it comes to the world ending, satan being defeated and casted into the lake of fire, and him manifesting his kingdom here but some of his promises are conditional that require you to do your part as well (when it comes to the destiny that he has for you, your salvation in order to get to heaven, and anything else that he's promised you so far etc.) Salvation is conditional because it requires you to abide in the spirit and not in the flesh, sacrifice idols, repentant sin, a relationship with him and to take up your cross and follow him.

Salvation is not only God's promise for man to come to repentance so that they can inherit the kingdom of God but it's also man's promise as well in order to get back home (your home which is heaven) but do God forces anything to come to pass or anyone to choose him (which is their salvation) and his will, no he doesn't otherwise it isn't a relationship. A lot of churches preach religion and not relationship! The pastors preach to you that if you don't choose God you're going to hell; which is true but what's motivation and intent behind it: are some of his promises require you to also do your part as well Some of his promises are conditional and some are not! For example, some of God's general promises are unconditional: (when it comes to the Anti-Christ, the tribulation period, the world ending, satan being defeated, and him manifesting his kingdom here etc.) But some of his promises are conditional that require you to do your part as well (when it comes to the destiny that he has for you, your salvation in order to get to heaven, and anything else that he's promised you so far that require for you to do your part as well etc.) Another error that I see in Calvinism or Calvinistic religious beliefs is that they believe that God picks and chooses certain people that will go to hell and heaven this is also false doctrine as well. Just because Calvinist tell you that God foreknows everything and that he's omniscient (meaning the All knowing one) and that he can foresee if you're going to hell or not doesn't mean that you're not given free will to make a decision to work out your salvation with fear and trembling and go to heaven or stay in sin, not repentive of sin, and not abiding in Christ and go to hell. Yes, God can foresee if you're going to heaven or hell but you have to play your part as well too in order to obtain salvation. Calvinist believe in the false doctrine "once saved always saved." They believe that no matter what you did if God prechosen you for heaven then you're going to heaven and if you're going to hell then you're going to hell. If that was the case then why would ***(John 15:1-7)*** talks about Jesus being the true vine and man being the branch and if you continue abiding in him then you'll bear fruit for a branch can't bear fruit by itself and if any man doesn't abide in him and if they don't bear fruit then the branch is withered and the rest whom are not abiding in the vine are gathered together and thrown into the fire and they are burned. This is a parable of salvation and what salvation is. That's just goes to show you that your salvation is conditional. Even in the old testament the Israelites had salvation and it was conditional as well. As the new testament during the old testament salvation was promised to the people who had grace through faith in Christ; the old testament didn't gain salvation by the law because they couldn't keep the law. Animal sacrifices for forgiveness of sin didn't please God but faith in Christ gave them access to grace. To prove this, Paul points us to Abraham whom believed God, and it was credited to him as righteousness and the people who worked and who kept the law were under debt ***(Romans 4:1-5)***. Calvinist look at ***(Romans 8:27-28)*** and take it out of context because it says that, [28] *"And we know that all things work* *together for good to them that love God, to them who are the called according to his purpose.* [29] *"For whom he did foreknow, he also did* ***predestine*** *to be conformed to the image of his Son, that he might be the firstborn amoung many brethren."* I highlighted the word predestine because when Calvinist see that word they take it out of context and make it seem like God picks and chooses who's going to get saved and go to heaven and who's not when they're taking that scripture completely out of context and they're reading it from a carnal mind and not the mind of Christ. Anyone who's interpreting the bible from their carnal mind is wrong because the Holy Spirit has to lead you to read the bible and he has to teach you and break the scriptures down to you in order for you to receive the revelations of God for *the Holy spirit is your teacher* ***(John 14:26)***. Like I said earlier in this chapter, God's salvation is conditional for New testament believers just like it was for the Old testament believers and going back to the whole *true versus truth* concept. Yes, it may be true that God has predestine and made a path for us to get saved and to be conformed to the image of his son but do people choose him, no. Does God force people to choose him, no that's not God because it's all about a relationship with him and the Lord doesn't like for us to feel obligated to do anything because it's not his nature. Satan forces you to do stuff but God doesn't!!! Based on the promises that the Lord gives you like salvation for example are conditional and it requires you to do your part as well. God's general promises that are unconditional for example: (when it comes to the Anti-Christ, the tribulation period, the world ending, satan being defeated, and him manifesting his kingdom here etc.) nothing stands in God's general will but somethings that the Lord wants you to partake in requires your sacrifice of self-will and cooperation in order to bring that thing to pass. That about sums that up so God doesn't pick and choose who's going to go to heaven or hell just because he can foresee, it's up to man to do their part as well. Another false doctrine that the Calvinist believe in is that God picks and chooses certain people whom are called to ministry, this is also false doctrine. God chooses everybody, and if you're a Christian and you have the Holy Spirit you are called to ministry so seek the Lord in what he wants to use you for, but the thing is you have to go through the same process that Jesus did (which is go through a season of trial and testing in the wilderness season) in order to walk into your calling. Calvinist who teach you that God picks and chooses certain people who are called to ministry are lying to you. For ***(John 14:12)*** tells us that, *"Very truly I tell you, whoever **believes** in me will do the works I have been doing, and they will do even greater things than these, because I am going to the father."* In the book of Acts when the early church first got started Peter, John, and the other disciples went to Jerusalem to preach the gospel of Jesus Christ in order to make disciples. When the day of the Pentecost came they were all on one accord and in one place. Then the Holy Ghost came upon them and they started speaking in tongues as the spirit gave them utterance and filled with the Holy Ghost.

To make a long story short, everyone who was there question where did the tongues come from and Peter stood up and told them that it was prophesied by ***Joel*** that the signs and wonders would happen through the power of the Holy Spirit.
(Joel 2:28-32) [28] *"And it shall come to pass afterward*
That I will pour out My Spirit on all flesh;
Your sons and your daughters shall prophesy,
Your old men shall dream dreams,
Your young men shall see visions.
[29] *And also on My menservants and on My maidservants*
I will pour out My Spirit in those days.
[30] *"And I will show wonders in the heavens and in the earth:*
Blood and fire and pillars of smoke.
[31] *The sun shall be turned into darkness,*
And the moon into blood,
Before the coming of the great and awesome day of the Lord.
[32] *And it shall come to pass*
That whoever calls on the name of the Lord
Shall be saved.
For in Mount Zion and in Jerusalem there shall be deliverance,
As the Lord has said,
Among the remnant whom the Lord calls. Peter told the people in the crowd the same thing that The Lord prophesied to Joel: *In the last days that God he will pour out his Spirit upon all flesh: and your sons and daughters shall prophesy, and your young men shall see visions, and your old men shall dream dreams. And on Jesus's servants and on his*

handmaidens, I will pour out in those of his Spirit and they shall prophesy: And he will show wonders in heaven above, and signs in the earth beneath. That's just goes to show you that the Lord is sovereign and he is in control of time and his prophetic timeline because he created time so therefore the Lord isn't bound to time. ***(Acts 2:17-19)*** After hearing all of what Peter had said they asked him what shall they do and Peter told them to repent and be baptized every one of you in the name of Jesus Christ for the remission of sins, and you shall receive the gift of the Holy Ghost. Sure enough, they believed him and did as he said and thousands were baptized, added to the kingdom, and received the Holy Ghost and the fear of God came upon every soul and many signs and wonders were done by the apostles and they were on one accord. They were sharing the same doctrine (no division or denominations), had fellowship, breaking bread and saying prayers, they also sold their possessions and goods and parted them to all men who were in need and they were on one accord. ***(Acts 2:37-47)*** Do you see that today, no! This is how Satan can keep the Christians from operating in the power of God and from operating in their full identity as a Christian through *false Calvinistic beliefs, satanic philosophies* (**'Do what thou wilt'** meaning: ***Do what you want to do, peruse your own goals and aspirations without the approval of God and be your own god***), and *getting pastors to discard the Holy Spirit in churches when it comes to* ***the gifts, signs, miracles, and wonders***.

We are to be like the early church and we are to do greater things than what Jesus did and the fact that you don't see that today is very pathetic because all we have now is tradition, churchianity (it's not Christianity), a body of believers who are divided with different denominations and beliefs who don't believe certain scriptures about casting out demons, performing the signs and the wonders, don't believe that we can be perfect, and who are afraid to preach against sin and judgement. This is clearly not God and we aren't to be divided as Christians for we are one body and (1st Corinthians 12:12-13) tells us that. We are to be on one accord and in agreement and if we don't have that then we don't have fellowship. Now that about sums all of that up about the false Calvinistic beliefs, being in fellowship with another Christian, 'Do what thou wilt' and the meaning behind it. I hope you guys enjoy the third chapter of this book and I'll see you when you flip this page over to the next chapter of this book (which is chapter four). Thank you for reading this chapter and God bless you brethren!!!

CHAPTER FOUR

Signs and confirmations

When I first came to the Lord I already knew what we were supposed to be doing as disciples in Christ because when I was younger before I got saved I used to watch some Christian movies and I saw how to early church was so I assumed that the early church was the original gospel of Jesus Christ. They performed many signs, wonders, miracles, healings and much more and you don't see any of that in this modern-day era because man is stuck on philosophy and Christians don't have enough faith to generate the power of God inside them because of their lack of faith in their identity. The bible tells us to *not allow man to deceive us through philosophy and vain deceit.* ***(Colossians 2:8)*** Christians allow this matrix system and the world to influence them on what a "Christian" should be like and they go from believing the authentic gospel to believing a pharisee modern day Jesus. Many other churches don't preach about the Holy Spirit and the power of having the Holy Spirit and they just discard it because they feel like it's not useful and that's an error for most churches because without the Holy Spirit then you technically don't have salvation. ***(Romans 8:9)*** tells us that whomever don't have the Spirit of God dwelling in them then they are none of his but they are sons of man instead of sons of God. What are sons of man?! ***Sons of man*** are people whom don't have the

Spirit of God dwelling inside of them and whom are bound to sin and the sin nature. ***Sons of God*** are people who do have the Spirit of God dwelling inside of them and are born again in the Spirit. We know where we should be as Christians when it comes to how the early church was when it came down to demonstrating the power of God and manifesting his kingdom in the earth realm but there aren't a lot of pastors teaching about that subject because they mostly believe that they're still sinners saved by grace (which is an oxymoron: either a person is a sinner or they're saved by grace) and they probably don't believe the Gospel themselves that's why they have a form of Godliness but don't have his power demonstrated through them ***(2nd Timothy 3:5)***. Pastors who teach you that the signs, miracles, healings, and wonders aren't for today are lying to you because of their unbelief in the Gospel so that's how they get to the point of discarding the Holy Spirit from their church because of their unbelief but the Lord wants to continue that process with us today the same way he did with the early church. The reason why we don't see the power of God as prominent as we should is because we truly don't have Christians who are willing to fully live a life of self-denial for the simple fact that you have some Christians who are still in the world pursing their own personal goals and aspirations outside of Gods will for their lives so that keeps them from fully walking into their full identity in the Lord. You can see in the book of Acts how the early church was when they first got started with continuing Jesus's ministry after he ascended into heaven: (They performed the signs, the wonders, the healings, the miracles, and much more that we don't know about etc.) The Lord also wants us to continue with the spiritual gifts that he gave us through the Holy Spirit which is: (***The word of wisdom, the word of knowledge, the gift of faith, the gift of healing, the working of miracles, the gift of prophecy, the gift of discerning spirits, divers kinds of tongues, interpretation of tongues*** etc. ***1st Corinthians 12:4-11***) When I first came to the faith, as a babe in Christ I believed in the word of God and I had more faith in the word of God than any average believer who's been in the Lord for years. The reason for my faith was because I saw movies about Jesus and the early church doing the signs, the wonders, the miracles, and the healings so it wasn't hard for me not to believe in the power of God. I remember one time where we didn't have any food in the house and the Lord did that purposely to show us how he could come through for us. During that time when we didn't have any food in the house I prayed the prayer of faith for the Lord to lead us to get some free food and afterwards he led us to go to a church. ***(Matthew 7:7)*** Says that, *"Ask and it will be given to you; seek and you will find; knock and the door will be opened to you."* However, my mother, my auntie, and I had to go to a ministry called *The Cooperative Ministry* located on *3821 West Beltline Belevard, Columbia SC* for their assistance so they could help us pay rent for our home first before we could go to the church that the Lord led us to. Walking inside the Cooperative Ministry felt like heaven to me because when I first walked inside of the building I could feel the presence of God there so strong and when I went to go set down the Lord told me to look outside the window and look across the street and show enough he told me, *"That's the church you're going to get food from."* That was my first confirmation! The name of the church that I was going to get food from was called *St. John Baptist Church* right across from *The Cooperative Ministry* which was where I was at during the time before we went across the street to go ask for some food. Before we went across the street to go get some food my mom was called from her chair by an assistant from the Cooperative Ministry and they went in the back to go handle some business on how to pay the rent because it was due. After they were done taking care of business we were about to leave but before we left an elderly lady sitting across from us have us a blue ticket to help us get free food from the church across from us she told my mother to go around towards the back of the church where the playground was at and go through the first two double doors on her left when she first got there and the people at the church will assist her and give her free food so we did exactly that. The elderly lady was my second confirmation from God! As we went around the church towards the back of the church my auntie parked in a free parking space while my mother went to go inside to go get some food. I sat in the car with my auntie! Sitting in the car I felt an extreme level of peace in my spirit from God and I was shocked and amazed on how the Lord did that. He came through just like he said he would praise God!!! While me and my auntie were waiting for my mother to come out with a bag full of groceries we saw an elderly couple and his wife coming out with a bag full of food and I was amazed on how the Lord came through for them. They seemed like they were in love with each other and they had a huge grin on their faces. The husband helped his wife put the groceries in the back of the trunk, put the buggy back inside of the church and went straight home. In my Spirit I told the Lord, *"Thank you Lord for providing for me when I didn't have the money to provide for my family."* He (The Lord) replied to me, *"Nothings too hard for God!!!"* with a grin on his face. A couple of minutes later I saw my mom came out with a bag full of groceries and I jumped up and down inside the car then went outside to help my mother put the groceries inside of the trunk. The Lord is a provider because his name is, *I AM!!!* He's everything, The Alpha and Omega, The Great I AM, He's Omniscient (All-knowing), Omnipotent (All-powerful), and he's Omnipresent (Everywhere) the Lord is everything you could ever imagine and he's not in a religious box at all that people like to put him in he can do what he wants to do. Another miracle that the Lord did for us was off the wall. One morning, when my mother was taking my siblings to school that day I was on the computer typing up a book that the Lord put on my heart to do and I was telling him how I couldn't wait to see how you're going to come through for us during the tribulation period because that's what he was talking to me about while I was typing and then all of a sudden, the lights went out and the computer cut off. My first instinct was to pray because I knew that the Lord was trying to test my faith to see if I would trust him or not. So I did and he told me to use the authority that he's been given to me and I obeyed and I told the Lord to cut on the lights in the name of Jesus and all of a sudden, a couple of seconds passed and the lights cut back on. After that I was shocked on how the Lord did that and it boosted my faith in the Lord so much more. What's the moral of the story you guys? The moral of the story is that God wants people to trust him and stop feeling the need to labor all of the time just because you hear religious people say, *"Well the bible says if you don't work then you don't eat."* ***(2nd Thessalonians 3:10)*** when they're taking that scripture completely out of context. Yes, we know that the bible says that if we don't work then we don't get to eat but then again, you can't deny other testimonies where God has taken people through a season of wilderness to where they didn't have any money at all and God just wanted to teach them how he was going to bless them in abundance due to them having faith in him. If it's God's will for you to work then he'll lead you where to go and that's that but if he doesn't want you to work then just chill and rest in God's will. For example, a guy named Phil who was from California drove all the way to FIJI because a brother in Christ named Christopher wanted him to go to FIJI (This was in late December 2016). And ten days before Christopher went to FIJI God told Phil to go to FIJI. At first, Phil started to reason with the Lord because he walked by sight instead of trusting the Lord. Phil said, "Well Lord I don't have any money." And the Lord said again, "Go to FIJI!!!" Then Phil said again, "I don't have any money where am I going to find it." Then the Lord said again, "Go to FIJI!!!" As you can see the Lord isn't a logical God, he's a supernatural out of the box God and he isn't politically correct. So anyways, Phil went to FIJI and in Los Angeles Phil met up with Chris and sure enough they went to FIJI. When they got to FIJI Phil said that he was $1,648.00 short of money so what he did was when he got there he had switches mattresses and as he was switching mattresses he saw his wallet at the edge of the bed so he picked up the wallet but then he realized it wasn't his wallet because his wallet was in his back pocket so then when Phil opened up the wallet he found at the edge of the bed it had no identification in it but it was full on money. The money was exactly what he needed which was 1,648.00 dollars and more. What an amazing God we serve!!! The Lord really does provide for us and he really does care about the simple things that we whine and complain to him about. People doubt the hand of the Lord and lean unto their own understanding thinking that the Lord is a liar because they don't understand the way that God operates. The Lord isn't going to give you something without testing your faith with the thing that he promised you, and he can see if your heart has true faith when it comes to the thing that he promised you. It's good to have faith but at the same time you have to do what he's instructing you to do and if you fail you comply with him then you're not going to get the blessings that he has for you. The bible says that, "Faith without works is dead." ***(James 2:26)*** Faith is you stepping out on what the Lord told you to do; not you stepping ahead of God on what he told you not to do. Faith and works goes together and you can't have one without the other but if it's not God's will, if he doesn't confirm that thing to you (whatever it is that God has promise you) then it'll be wise to not move out of God's command. People who define faith as you just stepping out and doing something on your own terms obviously don't understand God's sovereignty and how he operates and I call these the ***faith steppers***. The faith steppers are the Christians who are very passionate and bold so they are the ones who like to rush ahead of God after they get their sign or confirmation from him and hope that he'll follow them there or some faith steppers act in self-will hoping that whatever they choose to do in this life or whatever they choose to peruse is God's will for their life (which is false doctrine and it's a form of 'Do what thou wilt'.) The faith steppers are the Christians who are more lenient towards the works aspect due to "faith" (or their definition of what faith is.) Let me give you guys an example, Abraham! In this scenario with Abraham ***(Genesis 15:16-21)*** God promised that he was going to give him the land but the iniquity of the Amorites is not yet full and the Lord made a covenant with Abraham saying "Unto thy seed have I given this land, from the river of Egypt unto the great river, the river Euphrates: The Kenites, and the Kenizzites, and the Kadmonites, and the Hittites, and the Perizzites, and the Rephaims, and the Amorites, and the Canaanites, and the Girgashites, and the Jebusites." God waited at a specific time to bring judgment on the Amorites because of their sins and after he brought judgement on the Amorites then Abraham could possess the land. Now what would've happened if Abraham would've went outside of God's permission and leading to go purse the land that he promised to him? Some bad things would've happened! Instead Abraham waited on God's timing and he got the land promised to him. Christians who are faith steppers that like to rush ahead of God and do their own thing are not walking in God's will for their life. On the other hand, you've got other believers that like to wait on the Lord's timing and confirmation for them to move and these are called the ***faith resters.*** The faith resters rest's in God's sovereignty and they understand God from a sovereign standpoint: They wait for confirmation from the Lord, they wait on his timing for them to go, and when he confirms that he wants them to go then they go. I stand in category number two: *The faith resters*!!! Whenever I pray to the Lord about something, he confirms it 100% either through one of his prophets on YouTube or through a dream or vision he gives me (if it's a dream I like to write my dreams down and later on the Holy Spirit goes over it with me.) Otherward, I rest in God's sovereignty and we as believers are really supposed to be led by the spirit of God in all things for ***(Romans 8:14)*** tells us that. Category one believers which are the *faith steppers* don't understand that.

It's common sense!!! We are God's flock and we are his sheep and if you look at a nature of a sheep, they're dumb animals so that should tell you that they need a Sheppard. Sheep's don't lead themselves the Sheppard leads them and without the Sheppard the sheep's have no guidance. The Lord is our Sheppard so it common sense that we should follow him! I don't see how Christians rationalize this to where we can pick and choose what we want to do with our lives and hope that God is going to follow us into what we want to do as believers of Christ. It doesn't work that way and that's pride on our part. Christians who do that are partaking in another gospel and another Jesus that isn't the Jesus of the bible and the Lord will cause that Christian to be deceived because of the idolatry that's in their heart and they don't want to hear, *"Thus saith the Lord!"* and wait on him for conformation they want to do what they want to do which is to be lied to and be told that's it's ok to still sin, party, smoke, be lukewarm, have sex, and live this careless lifestyle. The Lord will allow that prophet to prophecy falsely to them because of their disobedience and they didn't seek his will for their lives. This is what category one believers which are the faith steppers need to fear. Take Balaam as an example: The Lord allowed Balaam to be deceived because of his rebellion in ***(Numbers 22:1-35)***. If you're having trouble finding out whether if God wants you to do something then you need to seek him first. Scripture tells us that! ***(Matthew 6:33)*** *But seek ye first the kingdom of God, and his righteousness; and all these things shall be* *added unto you.* Faith steppers think that just because they read a certain scripture where it says: *God will give you the desires of your heart* ***(Psalms 37:4)*** but if you read that scripture fully it says that *if you* ***delight*** (meaning: To please someone greatly) *yourself also in the Lord, and he shall give you the desires of your heart.* The question is what is the condition of your heart? Is it full of idolatry or is it full of companionship for God's will and service? Whatever you have in your heart the Lord will give it to you based on what you have in your heart; this could be a good thing or a bad thing depending on what you have in your heart. A lot of Christians nowadays are hearing from a God that's answering their lusts that's full of idolatry because they don't want to seek his will for their lives. This should scare every believer and put the fear of God in every believer. Let's continue with scripture: ***(Psalms 37:5)*** *Commit your way to the LORD, trust also in Him, and He shall bring it to pass.* If you're not committing yourself to the Lord then he's not going to give that to you. It's important to seek his will in every aspect for your life. When it comes to scriptures and you want to know what scriptures to read for each day of the week you can cast lots. Before there was any such thing as "luck" whether it be good luck or bad luck there was casting lots. The definition of the word "luck" means: ***The chance happening of fortunate or adverse events.*** In the bible there's no mention of the word "luck" but there's such thing as a blessing and a curse ***(Deuteronomy 28:1-68)*** Ever decision is from the Lord like it says in ***(Proverbs 16:33)*** , there's a season for everything ***(Ecclesiastes 3:1-8),*** and why would scripture say that *life and death is in the power of the tongue* if there was a such thing as luck? ***(Proverbs 18:21)*** Casting lots are still biblical today the same as *casting out demons, having spiritual gifts through the Holy Spirit, and performing the signs and wonders* through those who still believe. (***Matthew 16:16-18)*** tells us this, "*[16] He who believes and is baptized will be* ***saved****; but he who does not believe will be condemned. [17] And these signs will follow those who believe: In My name they will cast out demons; they will speak with new tongues; [18] they will take up serpents; and if they drink anything deadly, it will by no means hurt them; they will lay hands on the sick, and they will recover."* The word *saved* translated in the Greek means *sozo* (which means to save, deliver, protect, heal, preserve, do well, and be made whole.) Any gospel that preaches to you that it's impossible for Jesus to deliver you from sin, make you whole (meaning being perfect like Christ) that person preaches a false gospel for we are to be perfect like Jesus like ***(Matthew 5:48)*** says. We've been given authority through Jesus Christ to cast out demons because we believe so therefore the signs and wonders shall follow. All of these apostate churches, and mega churches that tells you that the signs, the wonders, the miracles, and the healings aren't for today are lying to you. Now going back to talking about casting lots and what the purpose was for casting lots. ***Casting lots*** *was used to help with decision-making and they would flip coins to choose whether to go with plan A or plan*

B. We can cast lots even today to find out what God's will is for our lives but it's not a requirement because we have the Holy Spirit to guide is because he'll guide us into all truth. If you're led by the Holy Spirit to cast lots then you can it's not a big deal. For example, after Judas died due to the judgement of God because he betrayed Jesus the eleven disciples went back to Jerusalem to pick another disciple so they casted lots; but it was God's will for Judas to die because Jesus already foreknew who the son of perdition would be in ***(John 13:18-30)***. Peter talked about Judas's death and scripture being fulfilled from what king David had spoken in ***(Acts 1:16-20)***. It was a hundred and twenty people with them and it came down to two people: *Justus and Matthias*. When they casted lots it fell on Matthias and he was added along with the eleven disciples and this was from ***(Acts 1-21-26)***. Let's use a scenario for an example! Let's say you're a Christian and you want to find out what bible chapter God wants you to read. You would flip a coin and depending on which side the coin lands on (heads or tails) it's going to determine if you'll roll one dice or two dices. If the coin lands on heads you roll one dice; but if the coin lands on tails you roll two dices. After you toss a coin and it lands on heads then you'll have to roll one dice and if the dice lands on the number five for example then you'll have to read the book of Genesis to the book of Deuteronomy. Now if you flip a coin and it lands on tails then you'd roll two dices. Let's say one dice lands on the number two and the other dice lands on the number three then you'll read the book of Isaiah (which is the 23rd book of the bible). You can also cast lots to go over dreams that the Lord had you to write down for confirmation by the numbers of the dreams that he gave you from dream one through how many other dreams you had from the Lord. It's the same method for the same purpose to find out God's daily plan for you every day. For example, you flip a coin and it lands on heads you'll then again roll one dice and based on what number it rolls on is the dream you go through with the Lord by the number of that dream. If you flip a coin and it lands on tails then you'll roll two dices: if the first dice lands on the number two and the second dice roll on the number six then you'll go through dream number twenty-six. It's that simple!!! Now am I saying that you have to cast lots for the rest of your Christian walk to determine if it's God's will or not, no. The bible says, "*the Holy Spirit will guide you into all truth*" ***(John 16:13)*** You can just seek God yourself and the Holy Spirit will reveal to you what he wants you to do during your walk with the Lord and it's mainly his job to confirm to you what he wants you to do not casting lots but if the Holy Spirit leads you to cast lots then do it because it's still biblical today. Now let's talk about healing and miracles!!! One time I remember when I woke up with a pain in my right eye and boy was it burning so bad. I had a dry eye. I tried everything I could possibly think of and it failed me. I tried splashing water on my face (hoping that the water goes into my eyes since I didn't have any eye drops).

I tried going to sleep thinking that the pain was going to go away after having thirty minutes of sleep. I tried taking a break from looking on my phone and that didn't work and the Holy Spirit told me to call on the name of Jesus for your healing so I did. Repeatedly I called on the name of the father, "Jesus, Jesus, Jesus, Jesus, Jesus, Jesus!" The next thing you know my eye stopped hurting! I ran in my mother room and told her exactly what happened and she was amazed. Praise God! It's true everything that the word of God tells us is truth I don't see how people don't get it. ***(John 17:17)*** tells us that, *"Sanctify them through thy truth: thy word is truth."* The devil is the one who's whispering lies! It's impossible for God to lie because ***he's not a man that he shall lie. (Numbers 23:19)*** If God lies then he's not worthy to be God! People would rather stay in their sin, stay in infirmity, stay in their misery, stay in darkness, and stay tormented by spirits then accept the precious gift of Jesus Christ because he can give you better than what you want because the Lord knows what you need. That's why it's foolish for Christians to betray God to go back into the world because that's just goes to show they don't understand the gospel of Jesus Christ and what being a Christian actually intel's on. You literally got God's spirit inside of you and that's something that the majority of this world does not have. Now let's talk about how to hear the Lord's voice. I hear a lot of people ask the similar question within the body of Christ how do I hear the Lord's voice? It's simple you're his creator and he's your creator. You'll know when it's

God's trying to communicate something to you because you have the Holy Spirit and your spirit will bear witness to whatever the Lord is trying to communicate to you with. ***(John 10:27)*** *My sheep hear my voice, and I know them, and they follow me.* In order to know if you have the Holy Spirit your spirit will bear witness to the word of God when you read it. ***(Romans 8:16)*** *The Spirit itself beareth witness with our spirit, that we are the children of God.* The fruits of the spirit are: ***love, joy, peace, longsuffering, gentleness, goodness, faith, Meekness, temperance (Galatians 5:22-23)*** these are the fruits of the Holy Spirit that'll confirm if you have it or not; and if you have the Holy Spirit then you are the sons of God and if you don't have it then **you're none of his** ***(Romans 8:9)***. Sometimes the Lord will communicate something to you in picture form or what I like to call it thought form. What happens is when it's the Lord trying to communicate something to you then your spirit will bear witness with all of this information that God is trying to instill in you and it'll pop up in your mind as a thought. That's why it's important for us as Christians to renew our mind and stay in the word in order to stay in communion with God so he can download into us and speak to us about what he wants us to do. I've had experiences where the enemy would torment me about if I'm hearing God or not and I'll get discouraged on whether I heard the Lord tell me to do a specific thing because of the hinderance of my carnal mind (that's just goes to show you that *the carnal mind is enmity against God*. ***Romans 8:6-7***) Then after the enemy has tried to discourage me about whether or not if I heard from God then the Lord will faithfully communicate and confirm to me a second time about what he told me the first time. Take heed the enemy will have you to doubt God by challenging your mind with philosophy the same way he did with Eve: *"Has God indeed said, 'You shall not eat of every tree of the garden'?"* ***(Genesis 3:1)*** Satan will attack your mind using reverse psychology and human reasoning because he knows that if he can get to your mind then he has you. The Lord on the other hand isn't a logical God nor is he politically correct, God speaks and it is so. ***(Ezekiel 12:25)*** *For I am the LORD: I will speak, and the word that I shall speak shall come to pass; it shall be no more prolonged: for in your days, O rebellious house, will I say the word, and will perform it, saith the Lord GOD.* This is how you can discern if it's God's speaking or it's the Lord speaking. Pay attention to how your spirit is bearing witness to that thing.

CHAPTER FIVE

Deception

A lot of Christians are falling for the great deception because their either still in sin or they just don't love the truth. The great deception has arrived and it's to separate the wheat from the tares. The true Christians from the lukewarm Christians and the holy from the heathen. The bible says in, ***(1st Timothy 4:1)*** that, *"Now the Spirit speaketh expressly, that in the latter times some shall depart from the faith, giving heed to seducing spirits, and doctrines of devils;*

2 Speaking lies in hypocrisy; having their conscience seared with a hot iron." It's a lot of false doctrine out there you guys when it comes to Christianity and most of the false doctrine comes from doctrines of devils and demons so it's a variety of different doctrines of devils but I'm only going to elaborate on a few. One false doctrine that most Christians participate in are paganistic holidays. In denominational churches, they celebrate these holidays like they were God given especially the holiday of Christmas. You hear a lot of religious folk tell you that December the 25th was the birth of Jesus Christ and that he created Christmas (which is a lie, the same way tithes and offerings are a lie because it isn't for new testament believers.) If you read scripture then you would know that Jesus wasn't born on December the 25th.

(Luke 2:7-8) *And she brought forth her firstborn son, and wrapped him in swaddling clothes, and laid him in a manger; because there was no room for them in the inn.*

8 *And there were in the same country* ***shepherds abiding in the field, keeping watch over their flock by night***. If Jesus was born on December the 25th during the winter time then what were the shepherds doing abiding in the field in the night time watching over the sheep's whom were also on the field with the shepherds? If it was winter then the shepherd wouldn't be outside watching the sheep's then and that's just goes to show you that Jesus wasn't born during the winter time he was born somewhere in the season of fall. December the 25th was the birth of Nemrod (which was a statue god and it was the most powerful statue god for sun worship. In other wards a graven image is a demonic and cursed object.) This is another scripture that supports the second reason why the Lord doesn't want us participating in Christmas. ***(Jeremiah 10:1-15)*** *Hear ye the word which the Lord speaketh unto you, O house of Israel:*

2 *Thus saith the Lord, Learn not the way of the heathen, and be not dismayed at the signs of heaven; for the heathen are dismayed at them.*

3 *For the customs of the people are vain: for one cutteth a tree out of the forest, the work of the hands of the workman, with the axe.*

4 *They deck it with silver and with gold; they fasten it with nails and with hammers, that it move not.*

5 *They are upright as the palm tree, but speak not: they must
needs be borne, because they cannot go. Be not afraid of
them; for they cannot do evil, neither also is it in them to do
good.*
6 *Forasmuch as there is none like unto thee, O Lord; thou art
great, and thy name is great in might.*
7 *Who would not fear thee, O King of nations? for to thee
doth it appertain: forasmuch as among all the wise men of
the nations, and in all their kingdoms, there is none like unto
thee.*
8 *But they are altogether brutish and foolish: the stock is a
doctrine of vanities.*
9 *Silver spread into plates is brought from Tarshish, and gold
from Uphaz, the work of the workman, and of the hands of
the founder: blue and purple is their clothing: they are all
the work of cunning men.*
10 *But the Lord is the true God, he is the living God, and an
everlasting king: at his wrath the earth shall tremble, and the
nations shall not be able to abide his indignation.*
11 *Thus shall ye say unto them, The gods that have not made
the heavens and the earth, even they shall perish from the
earth, and from under these heavens.*
12 *He hath made the earth by his power, he hath established
the world by his wisdom, and hath stretched out the heavens
by his discretion.*

13 *When he uttereth his voice, there is a multitude of waters
in the heavens, and he causeth the vapours to ascend from
the ends of the earth; he maketh lightnings with rain, and
bringeth forth the wind out of his treasures.*
14 *Every man is brutish in his knowledge: every founder is
confounded by the graven image: for his molten image is
falsehood, and there is no breath in them.*
15 *They are vanity, and the work of errors: in the time of their
visitation they shall perish.* The reason why people still celebrate these holidays is because they still look up to man to preach to them the gospel instead of the Holy Spirit. The bible says that *people are destroyed from a lack of knowledge* ***(Hosea 4:6)*** and it true we are destroyed from a lack on knowledge. We already know that Santa isn't real so that should tell you something about the holiday. If you rescramble the words "Santa" you get "Satan" you guys this isn't a joke. Christmas developed as a mean of replacing worship of the sun with worship of the Son (Jesus Christ). By 529 A.D after Christianity had become the official state religion of the Roman Empire, Emperor Justinian made Christmas a holiday. This is traditions of men!!! ***(Matthew 15:9)*** *But in vain they do worship me, teaching for doctrines the commandments of men.* All of these paganistic holidays stems from Rome and it mainly comes from the Roman Catholic church and you already know they worship the mother Mary instead of Jesus Christ and that is considered idolatry so you know their religion fake. That puts the icing on the cake, let's talk about another false doctrine: OSAS.

Also known as: Once saved always saved! I already elaborated on once saved always saved before you got to this chapter but I'm going to elaborate on it a little bit more. Once saved always saved means that all you have to do is say a sinner's prayer and your sins are covered for the past, present, and future and no matter what you do you're going to heaven. That is a lie from the pit of hell and that's not what the bible says. The bible says to w*ork out your salvation with fear and trembling* ***(Philippians 2:12)*** and *those who endure till the end shall be saved*. ***(Matthew 24:13)*** In order to get saved this is what you have to do: "*if you confess with your mouth and believe within your heart (about the gospel of Jesus Christ including the birth and resurrection) then you shall be saved*. ***(Romans 10:9)*** You're not saved by saying a sinner's prayer! After you made that declaration unto God you have to get baptized in the name of Jesus Christ and you'll receive the Holy Spirit. *The Holy Spirit is your helper sent from God to guide you unto holiness and to be transformed into the image of Jesus Christ.* ***(John 14:26)*** *The Holy Spirit will guide you unto all truth.* ***(John 16:13)*** You don't need no man to teach you the gospel of Jesus Christ you have the anointed one in you to teach you the gospel of Jesus Christ and you are the church; not a physical church building because the kingdom of God is within you so you need to bring the church to them. If you do sin, *you must confess your sin unto God and he'll cleanse you from all unrighteousness*. ***(1st John 1:9)***

Now does that mean that you are a slave to sin, no. For Paul said in ***(Romans 6:1-23)*** *What shall we say then? Shall we continue in sin, that grace may abound?*
2 God forbid. *How shall we, that are dead to sin, live any longer therein?*
3 *Know ye not, that so many of us as were baptized into Jesus Christ were baptized into his death?*
4 *Therefore we are buried with him by baptism into death: that like as Christ was raised up from the dead by the glory of the Father, even so we also should walk in newness of life.*
5 *For if we have been planted together in the likeness of his death, we shall be also in the likeness of his resurrection:*
6 *Knowing this, that our old man is crucified with him, that the body of sin might be destroyed, that henceforth we should not serve sin.*
7 *For he that is dead is freed from sin.*
8 *Now if we be dead with Christ, we believe that we shall also live with him:*
9 *Knowing that Christ being raised from the dead dieth no more; death hath no more dominion over him.*
10 *For in that he died, he died unto sin once: but in that he liveth, he liveth unto God.*
11 *Likewise reckon ye also yourselves to be dead indeed unto sin, but alive unto God through Jesus Christ our Lord.*
12 *Let not sin therefore reign in your mortal body, that ye should obey it in the lusts thereof.*
13 *Neither yield ye your members as instruments of unrighteousness unto sin: but yield yourselves unto God, as*

those that are alive from the dead, and your members as
instruments of righteousness unto God.
14 *For sin shall not have dominion over you: for ye are not*
under the law, but under grace.
15 *What then? shall we sin, because we are not under the law,*
but under grace? God forbid.
16 *Know ye not, that to whom ye yield yourselves servants to*
obey, his servants ye are to whom ye obey; whether of sin
unto death, or of obedience unto righteousness?
17 *But God be thanked, that ye were the servants of sin, but*
ye have obeyed from the heart that form of doctrine which
was delivered you.
18 *Being then made free from sin, ye became the servants of*
righteousness.
19 *I speak after the manner of men because of the infirmity of*
your flesh: for as ye have yielded your members servants to
uncleanness and to iniquity unto iniquity; even so now yield
your members servants to righteousness unto holiness.
20 *For when ye were the servants of sin, ye were free from*
righteousness.
21 *What fruit had ye then in those things whereof ye are now*
ashamed? for the end of those things is death.
22 *But now being made free from sin, and become servants to*
God, ye have your fruit unto holiness, and the end
everlasting life.
23 *For the wages of sin is death; but the gift of God is eternal*
life through Jesus Christ our Lord. Aslong as you're yielding
to the Holy Spirit and your abiding in the spirit then you're

not bound to sin; but if you're in your flesh you're still not bound to sin you choose to be in sin. Once you take your eyes off of Christ and stop abiding in the spirit then you'll start yielding to the lust of the flesh and you'll keep backsliding until you repent, take up your cross and follow Jesus again. This is how false doctrines are created and this is why majority of the Christian community as a whole believe that we're still bound to sin or they believe that we're just sinners saved by grace. Which is an oxymoron! Either a person is a sinner or he's saved by grace there's no such thing as both. The reason why a lot of Christians are dealing with the same thing is because they're not taking their walk with the Lord seriously. They don't go into warfare with prayer and fasting, they don't want to get self-deliverance or deliverance from evil spirits, they don't want to fully commit their life to the Lord and this is why they believe in the false doctrine once saved always saved because they're lukewarm. Let me give you guys scripture! ***(Galatians 5:1-26)*** *Stand fast therefore in the liberty wherewith Christ hath made us free, and be not entangled again with the yoke of bondage.*

2 Behold, I Paul say unto you, that if ye be circumcised, Christ shall profit you nothing.

3 For I testify again to every man that is circumcised, that he is a debtor to do the whole law.

4 Christ is become of no effect unto you, whosoever of you are justified by the law; ye are fallen from grace.

5 For we through the Spirit wait for the hope of righteousness by faith.

*6 For in Jesus Christ neither circumcision availeth any thing,
nor uncircumcision; but faith which worketh by love.
7 Ye did run well; who did hinder you that ye should not obey
the truth?
8 This persuasion cometh not of him that calleth you.
9 A little leaven leaveneth the whole lump.
10 I have confidence in you through the Lord, that ye will be
none otherwise minded: but he that troubleth you shall bear
his judgment, whosoever he be.
11 And I, brethren, if I yet preach circumcision, why do I yet
suffer persecution? then is the offence of the cross ceased.
12 I would they were even cut off which trouble you.
13 For, brethren, ye have been called unto liberty; only use
not liberty for an occasion to the flesh, but by love serve one
another.
14 For all the law is fulfilled in one word, even in this; Thou
shalt love thy neighbour as thyself.
15 But if ye bite and devour one another, take heed that ye be
not consumed one of another.
16 This I say then, Walk in the Spirit, and ye shall not fulfil
the lust of the flesh.
17 For the flesh lusteth against the Spirit, and the Spirit
against the flesh: and these are contrary the one to the other:
so that ye cannot do the things that ye would.
18 But if ye be led of the Spirit, ye are not under the law.
19 Now the works of the flesh are manifest, which are these;
Adultery, fornication, uncleanness, lasciviousness,*

[20] *Idolatry, witchcraft, hatred, variance, emulations, wrath,*
strife, seditions, heresies,
[21] *Envyings, murders, drunkenness, revellings, and such like:*
of the which I tell you before, as I have also told you in time
past, that they which do such things shall not inherit the
kingdom of God.
[22] *But the fruit of the Spirit is love, joy, peace, longsuffering,*
gentleness, goodness, faith,
[23] *Meekness, temperance: against such there is no law.*
[24] *And they that are Christ's have crucified the flesh with the*
affections and lusts.
[25] *If we live in the Spirit, let us also walk in the Spirit.*
[26] *Let us not be desirous of vain glory, provoking one*
another, envying one another. So if you walk according to the flesh then you're going to manifest the things of the flesh but if you walk according to the spirit then you're going to manifest the fruit of the Spirit it's that simple. You've got to want it. The false grace that most preachers talk about is: Sin all you want you'll never be perfect, just died to pay for all sin so don't worry about it. The true definition of grace that Paul talks about is having liberty from sin just like he said in ***(Galatians 5:1)*** The Lord gives you grace to stop sinning through the power of the Holy Spirit and when you're spending time with God, in his word, and you're in intimacy with God those desires start to drift away. Especially when you have the Holy Spirit in you it'll be hard to just do what you want to do because once you get the Spirit of God inside of you he's going to convict you of sin and it's going to feel

like a heavy burden on your shoulder once you try to continue going back towards your vomit that you spat up. You'll feel the conviction so strong it'll make you turn around from sin and if you do sin the guilt that the Holy Spirit gives you is going to bring you back to repentance and then he'll leave you alone and that is called ***conviction***. The Lord doesn't play! If you choose to disobey God and go sin anyway the Lord is going to deliver you unto the hand of Satan (to where Satan torments you) until you repent to God. Even after you repent the enemies going to place a false guilt on you and try to make you feel guilty for your sin immediately after you repent to God or a couple of days later from when you repented where you're doing something and Satan brings the sin back up in your face out of the blue. This my friend is called ***condemnation***! ***(Romans 8:1)*** says this, "There is therefore now no **condemnation** to them which are in Christ Jesus, who walk not after the flesh, but after the Spirit." If the enemy is condemning you of your sin that isn't of God (clearly, it's not of God) but just know that after you've repented from your sin God has forgiven you and the conviction of the Holy Spirit stops unless you go back to sinning or yield to the lust of your flesh that's a whole different story pal. The Father, the Son, and the Holy Spirit are one and apart from God giving you his Holy Spirit is to transform you back into the image of your creator; from how you were before the fall of Adam and Eve. God's trying to restore your relationship with him because he loves you so much and he wants you to be transformed into his son's image (which is Jesus Christ through the Holy Spirit). The Holy Spirit is your helper to help you be transformed into the image of God because you were made in his image and he want's that to be restored again; but the sin of Adam and Eve caused us to fall from God's grace so therefore we couldn't mimic our creator anymore because of that. In Adam, we all died because he gave dominion to Adam not Eve; imagine if Eve would've sinned and not Adam then God probably would've restored her through Adam but it wasn't God's divine plan so through Jesus Christ, we're made alive unto God again. For scripture tells us so. ***(1st Corinthians 15:22)*** *For as in Adam all die, even so in Christ shall all be made alive.* People don't tell you once you get saved you've been brought with a price in ***(1st Corinthians 6:20)*** so really, it's not about your life anymore it's about God's will for your life now. You have to seek first the kingdom of heaven for what you want to do with your life because God already has his plans mapped out for you so ask him to reveal them to you. That covers most false doctrine that these apostate pastors preach! Another form of deception is NASA and you'd think that NASA stands for: ***National Aeronautics and Space Administration*** but if you look up the word "NASA" in Hebrew it means to deceive people. NASA believes in geometry! Gematria (in Greek: meaning geometry) is an Assyro-Babylonian-Greek system of code and numerology later adopted into Jewish culture that assigns numerical value to a word or phrase in the belief that words or phrases with identical numerical values bear some relation to each other or bear some relation to the number itself as it may apply to nature, a person's age, the calendar year or the like.

CHAPTER SIX

Religion versus Relationship

The Lord doesn't want us following religion because religion is man-made the Lord wants a relationship with you and me. Religion puts God in a box when he's not in a box at all, where the Spirit of God is there's liberty. Because God is free he wants you to be free as well. Because God is free he wants you to be free as well. Where the Spirit of the Lord is there's liberty (2nd Corinthians 3:17) meaning that the Lord will never lead you to do something that's going to put you in bondage or lead you into sin because you're free from the law of sin and death. You may ask me, "Well what's the law of sin and death?" The law of sin and death was for people who were unrighteous (sinners) and who didn't want to walk with God because they were disobedient towards God so in the old testament under the law of Moses if someone was to do something against God depending on how bad the sin was they either got stoned and killed or got punished by God. There were sin offerings in the old testament as well when there were blood sacrifices of animals to be as an atonement for man's sin in order to be forgiven by God, but it also was a foreshadow of the ultimate blood sacrifice which was Jesus Christ God in the flesh dying for our sins. In the old testament it may seem like God was unmerciful, but he was only unmerciful to the tribes who served Babylonian gods (pagan gods) and who God already foreknew didn't want to repent. There was the mercy of God in the old testament as well according to [Ezekiel 33:16-26] and [Genesis 18:16-33] when God wanted Abraham to intercede for Sodom and Gomorrah, so the Lord wouldn't destroy it if he found ten righteous man so that just goes to show you that the Lord is merciful. The people who didn't have faith in God's word and who were unrighteous were judged under the law of sin and death because of their carnality and the Greek word for carnality is *Sarkikios* and it translates in the English as carnal, worldly, or culturally. This is why the bible tells us that the carnal mind is enmity against God [Romans 8:7]. People who didn't have faith in God's word in the old testament become an enemy towards God because of what Hebrews 11:6 and Revelation 21:8 tells us that unbelief is sin therefore the unbelieving will go to hell because the kingdom of God is founded on faith and anything contrary to faith is antigod. In the old testament when the Israelites didn't have faith in God's word and then they were doubting they went after false gods causing them to sin and under the law of Moses if they went after false gods they automatically subjected themselves to the law of sin and death therefore God subtracted the unrighteous from the righteous this is why Romans 3:23 says for the wages of sin is death. But when Jesus came he freed us from the law of sin and death by coming down as the word and God in the flesh living out the word of God in the flesh and become the curse for us so that we can be free from the law of sin and death this is why

Romans 8:1 is the foundation of the gospel. You don't try to obey the word of God through your own strength you first have to apply faith towards the word first [Romans 10:17] and as you do that the Holy Spirit is renewing your mind from a fleshly carnal mind of unbelief to belief, so he can live the word through you by abiding in Jesus's love. The word washes you as you read it, the Holy Spirit works on your mind to cleanse it from any contrary filthy thoughts that are of the devil and you start bearing fruit of the Spirit. This is why Jesus said in John 15:4-5, *"Remain in me and I will remain in you. No branch can bear fruit by itself it must remain in the vine. Neither can you bear fruit unless you remain in me. I am the vine; you are the branches. If any man remains in me and I in him he will bear much fruit; apart from me he can do nothing."* (NIV version) What are the fruits of the Spirit? ***Love, joy, peace, patience, kindness, goodness, faithfulness, gentleness, and self-control.*** [Galatians 5:22-23]

When God made Adam, he blew the breath of life inside of him and Adam became a living being. The Greek word for breath is *Pneuma* and Pneuma means Spirit. So, when God blew the breath of life into Adam he took on God's Spirit therefore being and walking as an exact replica of God: Righteous, Holy, Innocent, and without sin. Notice how I said before on how when God creates something or someone he gives us free will so the ability to rebel must exist also. When Satan caused Adam and Eve to fell the soul became out of sync with the Spirit of God therefore they couldn't no longer mirror the Father (God) and his nature Adam was the first son of God but when he fell he became the son of man the reason why he was the son of God was because he mirrored the likeness of God Adam was the first son of God. When Adam and Eve had kids, they took on the form and DNA of Adam and whatever sin that was in Adam transferred to his offspring's. On the other hand, Jesus came down from heaven and he had no nature or DNA of Adam in him instead he had the DNA of God in him because Jesus was the word made flesh in John 1:14 therefore Jesus was the second son of God. When Jesus died on the cross he took on our sin nature by become the curse for us and destroying the law of sin and death because he was the only one who could keep the law because he was the word made flesh. When he cried out to God on that cross the Lord rejected him, and heaven rejected him because our sins was transferred to the cross and under the blood of Jesus we transferred as sons of God through the blood of Jesus to be reborn again as sons of God taking back our original identity that God gave Adam before he fell. Notice how when one of the Roman soldiers went to go check to see if Jesus was dead he pierced his side and when the solider had pierced Jesus's side blood came out and it gushed out on his face and the romans solider became redeemed that was because Jesus had the blood of God in him because he was God's son and he had no DNA of Adam in him. So, what I'm basically implying is that you need to get under the blood of Jesus and you'll take on the nature of God by reading the word of God and it washes away any filth and DNA of Adam that came from Adam's offspring.

- Ask Jesus to forgive you of your sins and cleanse you from all unrighteousness by his blood so that you can take on the nature of God again. Ask God to feel you with his Holy Spirit to keep you Holy.
- Get into the word because the word is the seed that's being planted and when you're communing with Jesus the seed starts to grow, and you bear fruit.

Hearing God's voice

Nobody can teach you how to hear God's voice because it first nature when you become born again the only thing that keeps you from hearing God's voice is sin and you not taking heed to the urging of the Spirit of God (Holy Spirit). Jesus says my sheep know my voice in John 10:4 so if you're truly a part of his flock then you will know his voice. One way to know the Lord's voice is when you talk to him in your mind something will resonate in your spirit man or spirit woman and a thought will pop up in your mind and it'll bear witness with your Spirit. God can speak audibly but it's only through dreams and visions when Apostle Peter was on a flat roof praying it was about noon and he was hungry, so he fell into a trance and the voice of God spoke to him, *"Get up, Peter; kill and eat them"*. [Acts 10:9-13] God can also speak through scripture and most Christians call it an rhema word. A *rhema word* is basically an utterance from the Holy Spirit leading or guiding you through scripture, words of knowledge about someone or something confirming something that you prayed about etc. God can also speak to you through dreams as well and this is prophesied by the prophet Joel in Joel 2:28 an example that God speaks to you through dreams and visions is when Jesus was born an angel appeared to Joseph and told him to take the baby to Egypt because Herod was about to kill Jesus [Matthew 2:12-20] God can speak through prophets as well!!!

You can also have God give you a vision while you're awake if you have an seer gift which is another form of an prophet and a seer is someone who sees into the spirit realm whether it be a vision that the Lord wants to give them, or the Lord wants them to see spirits in the spirit realm he'll enable that seer to see spiritual things that are not there so prophets aren't just oracles for God they're seers as well. To also hearing God's voice, you must fast as well and fasting isn't you just fasting because you're trying to lose weight you're fasting because you're denying yourself to grow closer to God by reading his word, listening to praise and worship music, watching Christian video's that edify the Spirit. These are the types of fasts that you can do but you must seek the Holy Spirit for what kind of fast the Lord wants you to do.

- Water fast – No food, juice, just water [Caution] before you go on a water fast make sure that you're training your body for the fast and don't just jump into it trying to do a water fast for ten days for example work your way up towards the fast. One the first day working towards a water fast eat one light meal and by the end of the first day eat a full meal. On the second day working towards your fast choose what time you want to eat but it has to be a light meal like crackers and tuna or chicken noodle soup and grilled cheese because bread can stick to your stomach for days.
- Absolute fast – No food and no water

- Daniel's fast- Fruits, vegetables, juices etc. [Daniel 1:12] fast from 7am-6pm that's when you can break your fast and eat fruits and vegetables.

- Intermitting fasting- Fast around 7am-4pm and eat at a five hour window [4pm-9pm] then fast the next day for an whole day and after you wake up the next morning you can eat from about 7am-12pm then fast until 9pm then go to bed after you wake up the next morning fast for the whole day and when you wake up the next morning fast from 7am-4pm eat again at an five hour window and repeat the process and yes you can eat anything that doesn't contain too much calories.

- Partial fast- Give up at least one item of food. You fast from 7am-7pm a partial fast can be a water fast, Daniel's fast etc.

These are ways you can hear God's voice through fasting!!!

Growing up in a Christian home where we kept our Christian values like I said in the beginning of the book I knew about God but I didn't know him intimately. I knew about him religious wise when it came down to going to church but I didn't know he relationship wise. Before I got saved I felt like God had hated me because of my sin and I felt like I couldn't redeem myself because of my past.

I attended church every Sunday trying to work to gain God's heart and work my way up in order to gain salvation. That wasn't required for new testament believers. If you try to keep the law out of your own strength and your own righteousness then you'll fall and be held accountable for keeping the whole law of God. Paul talks about this in ***(Romans 3:19-20)*** *Now we know that what things soever the law saith, it saith to them who are under the law: that every mouth may be stopped, and all the world may become guilty before God.[20] Therefore by the deeds of the law there shall no flesh be justified in his sight: for by the law is the knowledge of sin.* What Paul was saying was that if anybody tries to keep the law out of their own strength shall not be justified before the Lord and that's what I was doing. I was trying to keep the commandments out of my own strength in order to please God not knowing that it was not pleasable towards God nor did my works give me salvation in order to get to heaven. ***(Ephesians 2:8-9)*** *[8] For by grace are ye saved through faith; and that not of yourselves: it is the gift of God:[9] Not of works, lest any man should boast.* People try to still keep the law of Moses or Torah out of their own strength and fleshly will apart from the Holy Spirit. They keep God's Laws religiously because of obligation not because they love YHWH and His commandments. We don't keep God's laws to be saved we keep God's laws because we are saved that's why the Israelites kept on sinning and going after false gods because our works couldn't please God and our flesh couldn't submit to the

Law of God so that's why the Lord had created a new covenant for us so that when we get born again and receive the Holy Spirit we are able to keep God's commandments because we're obeying God's laws through the empowerment of the Holy Spirit not just by trying to keep the Law of God out of our own strength. A lot of people try to keep the oral torah (which is the law of the elders who required circumcision as recorded in the first five books of the Hebrew scriptures from Genesis through Deuteronomy etc.) when that's no longer a requirement for us to do in order to inherit salvation, and a lot of people are trying to keep the sabbath religiously like the seventh day Adventist as a requirement for salvation and not from the heart but you can keep it if you want for celebrations best known as holydays you can keep the sabbath, feast days, and other holydays as well but it's the fact that those Holydays aren't a requirement for salvation and remember no animal sacrifices either because we've been freed from the law of sin offerings (for Christ was the ultimate sacrifice and the Passover lamb, and things of that nature so doing those things are no longer an obligation.) according to ***(Colossians 2:16-23)***. This is where Paul talks about not letting a man judge you according to the law of sin and death (meaning let no one judge you of celebrating these holy days as a requirement for salvation when it's interpreted to celebrate freely for remembrance of God's faithfulness etc.) *Let no man therefore judge you in meat, or in drink, or in respect of a holyday, or of the new moon, or of the sabbath days:*

17 *Which are a shadow of things to come; but the body is of Christ.*

18 *Let no man beguile you of your reward in a voluntary humility and worshipping of angels, intruding into those things which he hath not seen, vainly puffed up by his fleshly mind,*

19 *And not holding the Head, from which all the body by joints and bands having nourishment ministered, and knit together, increaseth with the increase of God.*

20 *Wherefore if ye be dead with Christ from the rudiments of the world, why, as though living in the world, are ye subject to ordinances,*

21 *(Touch not; taste not; handle not;*

22 *Which all are to perish with the using;) after the commandments and doctrines of men?*

23 *Which things have indeed a shew of wisdom in will worship, and humility, and neglecting of the body: not in any honour to the satisfying of the flesh.* Circumcision are no longer a requirement because they're under the law of the elders and it was nailed to the cross when Jesus died so circumcision no longer matter because of Jesus being our Passover lamb and that's why Jesus had to come and die in our place because we were imperfect. Jesus could live out the law not only because he was perfect but because he was the word in flesh. ***(John 1:1)*** *In the beginning was the Word, and the Word was with God,* ***and the Word was God***. What does that tell you, Jesus came to show us how to fulfill the law while living in corruptible flesh to show us that it could

be done by being empowered by the Holy Spirit and dying to the flesh by doing fasting and prayer. So, Jesus's mandate was to not only die for our sins but so that he could relate to what we were going through being trapped in a fleshly body. God is bound to his word and when I meant the term "bound to his word." I meant that God is subjected to his word that he can't lie because he's God and he's not a liar but the Lord isn't bound to the word when it comes to being a supernatural and being an out of box God intimate wise when it comes to your relationship with him. Jesus experienced what all of us struggled with but He overcame through the power of God and he made a way for us to do the same thing through the power of the Holy Spirit. You can't obey the word of God out of your own strength. This is the number one reason why sinners don't want to come to God because they believe that they first have to be perfect before they come to the Lord and that's a lie from the pit of hell. They have the conception of obeying the word of God out of their own strength when they're not capable of doing so because of their sin nature. We don't obey God's word out of our own strength and power we obey God's word through the Holy Spirit and intimacy spending time with the Lord. You need to get saved and receive the Holy Spirit in order to overcome sin. The Holy Spirit was the same thing that kept Jesus when he came down here to die for our sins and the same Spirit is there to help you overcome sin and be transformed into the image of Jesus Christ the way God first intended for us to be before the fall of Adam and Eve!

Religious people tell you that you have to be perfect in order for Christ to receive you but you notice that you're not perfect and what religious folk will do is make you feel bad about yourself like they weren't sinners at one point. God has mercy on everybody because he wants people to come to repentance and accept his son's sacrifice so that we can reign with him when it's time for him to collect his bride. God
desires for no man to perish! ***(1st Timothy 2:1-4)*** *I exhort*
therefore, that, first of all, supplications, prayers,
intercessions, and giving of thanks, be made for all men;
2 *For kings, and for all that are in authority; that we may*
lead a quiet and peaceable life in all godliness and honesty.
3 *For this is good and acceptable in the sight of God our*
Saviour; 4 ***Who will have all men to be saved, and to come***
unto the knowledge of the truth. Don't allow religious folk to push you away from God come as you are, for people in the bible who were used by God and the people that you see today whom are being used by God aren't better than you they just chose to accept God's salvation and submit to God's will for him to use them in a powerful way. Some people that God used like Solomon and David for example weren't perfect and they made mistakes and some mighty man of God like Paul was on fire for God and finished what God had in store for him. Some apostles will even admit to being imperfect in scripture let's go to ***(Titus 3:1-5)*** *Put them in mind to be subject to principalities and powers, to obey magistrates, to be ready to every good work,*

2 To speak evil of no man, to be no brawlers, but gentle, shewing all meekness unto all men.
3 For we ourselves also were sometimes foolish, disobedient, deceived, serving divers lusts and pleasures, living in malice and envy, hateful, and hating one another.
4 But after that the kindness and love of God our Saviour toward man appeared,
*5 Not by works of righteousness which we have done, but according to his mercy he saved us, by the washing of regeneration, and renewing of the **Holy Ghost**; Which he shed on us abundantly through Jesus Christ our Saviour;*
7 That being justified by his grace, we should be made heirs according to the hope of eternal life. The Holy Ghost is what kept them from sin so they could have a chance at eternal life. God doesn't want religion he wants a relationship with you because he paid a high price of given his son for our sins so that we could have a chance to get back home. He wants to know how your day was, God cares about you and your well-being, God wants to have a relationship with you just like you have a relationship with your family and friends. He's your creator so if he hated you then why would he sent his son to go die for your sins? ***(John 3:16)*** *For God so loved the world, that he gave his only begotten Son, that whosoever believeth in him should not perish, but have everlasting life.* The devil will allow circumstances and things to make you think that the Lord doesn't love you but the purpose that God has planned for you requires you to go through something in order for you to relate to other people

when the Lord finally promotes you to have you minister to people who lost faith in God. He did it with his twelve disciples! Jesus never sent out anyone to do ministry who didn't spend enough time with him. They had to walk with Jesus all the way even through the trials and tribulations. You have to be proven by God to receive the prosperity that he has for you and your faith has to be tested because it's always been that way from the start, he did the same thing with Joseph. God promised Joseph that he was going to be this great king amongst his brothers so Joseph told his brothers and his brothers got mad and threw him in jail because of the Lord's calling on his life. ***(Genesis 37:1-36)***
Jacob lived in the land of his father's sojournings, in the land of Canaan.
2 These are the generations of Jacob.
Joseph, being seventeen years old, was pasturing the flock with his brothers. He was a boy with the sons of Bilhah and Zilpah, his father's wives. And Joseph brought a bad report
of them to their father. 3 Now Israel loved Joseph more than
any other of his sons, because he was the son of his old age.
And he made him a robe of many colors. 4 But when his
brothers saw that their father loved him more than all his brothers, they hated him and could not speak peacefully to him.
5 Now Joseph had a dream, and when he told it to his
brothers they hated him even more. 6 He said to them, "Hear
this dream that I have dreamed: 7 Behold, we were binding
sheaves in the field, and behold, my sheaf arose and stood

upright. And behold, your sheaves gathered around it and
bowed down to my sheaf.” [8] His brothers said to him, “Are
you indeed to reign over us? Or are you indeed to rule over
us?” So they hated him even more for his dreams and for his
words.
[9] Then he dreamed another dream and told it to his brothers
and said, “Behold, I have dreamed another dream. Behold,
the sun, the moon, and eleven stars were bowing down to
me.” [10] But when he told it to his father and to his brothers,
his father rebuked him and said to him, “What is this dream
that you have dreamed? Shall I and your mother and your
brothers indeed come to bow ourselves to the ground before
you?” [11] And his brothers were jealous of him, but his father
kept the saying in mind.

Joseph Sold by His Brothers

[12] Now his brothers went to pasture their father's flock near
Shechem. [13] And Israel said to Joseph, “Are not your
brothers pasturing the flock at Shechem? Come, I will send
you to them.” And he said to him, “Here I am.” [14] So he said
to him, “Go now, see if it is well with your brothers and with
the flock, and bring me word.” So he sent him from the
Valley of Hebron, and he came to Shechem. [15] And a man
found him wandering in the fields. And the man asked him,
“What are you seeking?” [16] “I am seeking my brothers,” he
said. “Tell me, please, where they are pasturing the flock.”
[17] And the man said, “They have gone away, for I heard them
say, ‘Let us go to Dothan.’” So Joseph went after his
brothers and found them at Dothan.

*18 They saw him from afar, and before he came near to them
they conspired against him to kill him. 19 They said to one
another, "Here comes this dreamer. 20 Come now, let us kill
him and throw him into one of the pits. Then we will say that
a fierce animal has devoured him, and we will see what will
become of his dreams." 21 But when Reuben heard it, he
rescued him out of their hands, saying, "Let us not take his
life." 22 And Reuben said to them, "Shed no blood; throw
him into this pit here in the wilderness, but do not lay a hand
on him"—that he might rescue him out of their hand to
restore him to his father. 23 So when Joseph came to his
brothers, they stripped him of his robe, the robe of many
colors that he wore. 24 And they took him and threw him into
a pit. The pit was empty; there was no water in it.*

*25 Then they sat down to eat. And looking up they saw a
caravan of Ishmaelites coming from Gilead, with their
camels bearing gum, balm, and myrrh, on their way to carry
it down to Egypt. 26 Then Judah said to his brothers, "What
profit is it if we kill our brother and conceal his blood?
27 Come, let us sell him to the Ishmaelites, and let not our
hand be upon him, for he is our brother, our own flesh." And
his brothers listened to him. 28 Then Midianite traders passed
by. And they drew Joseph up and lifted him out of the pit,
and sold him to the Ishmaelites for twenty shekels[c] of silver.
They took Joseph to Egypt.*

*29 When Reuben returned to the pit and saw that Joseph was
not in the pit, he tore his clothes 30 and returned to his
brothers and said, "The boy is gone, and I, where shall I*

go?" 31 Then they took Joseph's robe and slaughtered a goat
and dipped the robe in the blood. 32 And they sent the robe of
many colors and brought it to their father and said, "This we
have found; please identify whether it is your son's robe or
not." 33 And he identified it and said, "It is my son's robe. A
fierce animal has devoured him. Joseph is without doubt torn
to pieces." 34 Then Jacob tore his garments and put
sackcloth on his loins and mourned for his son many days.
35 All his sons and all his daughters rose up to comfort him,
but he refused to be comforted and said, "No, I shall go
down to Sheol to my son, mourning." Thus his father wept
for him. 36 Meanwhile the Midianites had sold him in Egypt
to Potiphar, an officer of Pharaoh, the captain of the guard.
After Jospeh became king years after being locked up in
prison Jospeh confronted his brothers and told them, **"what
they meant for evil God meant for good."(Genesis 50:1-20)**
And Joseph fell upon his father's face, and wept upon him,
and kissed him.
2 And Joseph commanded his servants the physicians to
embalm his father: and the physicians embalmed Israel.
3 And forty days were fulfilled for him; for so are fulfilled the
days of those which are embalmed: and the Egyptians
mourned for him threescore and ten days.
4 And when the days of his mourning were past, Joseph spake
unto the house of Pharaoh, saying, If now I have found grace
in your eyes, speak, I pray you, in the ears of Pharaoh,
saying,

5 *My father made me swear, saying, Lo, I die: in my grave
which I have digged for me in the land of Canaan, there
shalt thou bury me. Now therefore let me go up, I pray thee,
and bury my father, and I will come again.*
6 *And Pharaoh said, Go up, and bury thy father, according
as he made thee swear.*
7 *And Joseph went up to bury his father: and with him went
up all the servants of Pharaoh, the elders of his house, and
all the elders of the land of Egypt,*
8 *And all the house of Joseph, and his brethren, and his
father's house: only their little ones, and their flocks, and
their herds, they left in the land of Goshen.*
9 *And there went up with him both chariots and horsemen:
and it was a very great company.*
10 *And they came to the threshingfloor of Atad, which is
beyond Jordan, and there they mourned with a great and
very sore lamentation: and he made a mourning for his
father seven days.*
11 *And when the inhabitants of the land, the Canaanites, saw
the mourning in the floor of Atad, they said, This is a
grievous mourning to the Egyptians: wherefore the name of
it was called Abelmizraim, which is beyond Jordan.*
12 *And his sons did unto him according as he commanded
them:*
13 *For his sons carried him into the land of Canaan, and
buried him in the cave of the field of Machpelah, which
Abraham bought with the field for a possession of a
buryingplace of Ephron the Hittite, before Mamre.*

14 *And Joseph returned into Egypt, he, and his brethren, and
all that went up with him to bury his father, after he had
buried his father.*
15 *And when Joseph's brethren saw that their father was
dead, they said, Joseph will peradventure hate us, and will
certainly requite us all the evil which we did unto him.*
16 *And they sent a messenger unto Joseph, saying, Thy father
did command before he died, saying,*
17 *So shall ye say unto Joseph, Forgive, I pray thee now, the
trespass of thy brethren, and their sin; for they did unto thee
evil: and now, we pray thee, forgive the trespass of the
servants of the God of thy father. And Joseph wept when they
spake unto him.*
18 *And his brethren also went and fell down before his face;
and they said, Behold, we be thy servants.*
19 *And Joseph said unto them, Fear not: for am I in the place
of God?*
20 *But as for you, ye thought evil against me; but God meant
it unto good, to bring to pass, as it is this day, to save much
people alive.* People don't know that the things that they go through everyday is for God to prepare them for something that he wants to use that person for and when you have a carnal mind it doesn't seem that way but that's exactly what it is.

If you don't have the mind of Christ with everything that you go through then you'll never have the victory that the Lord wants for you.

CHAPTER SEVEN

Demons and black magic

In the eastern part of the country of Africa they practice a lot of witchcraft and voodoo. Witchcraft and voodoo are part of indigenous African spirituality, and it is being mixed with Christianity and Islam today. For outsiders, (meaning westerners like America) that is hard to understand, but practitioners are very serious about their beliefs. The English word witchcraft refers to all sorts of sorcery and magic, often emphasizing destructive, evil intentions. The bible says that rebellion is as witchcraft ***(1st Samuel 15:23)*** *For rebellion is as the sin of witchcraft, and stubbornness is as iniquity and idolatry. Because thou hast rejected the word of the Lord, he hath also rejected thee from being king.* Any power that's been given to an individual outside of God and the Holy Spirit is witchcraft. Generally speaking, witchcraft appears to be more relevant in West Africa than in East Africa today, and there are great differences between countries and tribes. Witchcraft rituals are practiced in secrecy and often at night. If something tragic occurred as a result of practicing witchcraft and voodoo like for example, someone passes away the next day prior to a witch performing witchcraft and voodoo on that person then a witness would say, "That person was probably cursed by a witch." That's true!

On the other hand, if a citizen in America would've experience the same tragedy of a loved one dying without a cause they'll probably false accuse somebody for murder and get them thrown in jail because America is so carnal minded due to TV programming so much media they see on television. People don't even know the things that they partake in everyday is witchcraft. For example, when people smoke cigarettes and weed they are performing witchcraft on themselves. Where we get the word pharmacy from is from the Greek word *pharmikia* and the word *pharmikia* means **sorcery** and **witchcraft**. Witchcraft isn't just about a group of people standing in a dark room doing incantations around a pentagram and praying to Satan twenty-four hours. Witchcraft is the things we partake in everyday! Another example is when the media advertise materialistic things on television. The reason for this is because if you really knew where these things that you want come from you wouldn't be lusting after these things. I watched an ex voodooist testimony where he talked about when he was in the occult any chance, he got to go into the ocean to go into the spiritual realm he went. In the natural he said that it was the ocean but in the spiritual realm it was the marine kingdom of Satan. He talked about when he tapped into the spiritual realm he saw witch doctors and scientist in the spirit making materialistic things in the spirit like cars, jeweler, cosmetics, and other things to puff up your sin nature and they manifest it in the natural to subdue you and to keep you wanting their stuff that is known as the pride of life and idolatry.

This satanic theory is known as: ***<u>'As above so below'</u>*** The meaning *'As above so below'* is a similar meaning of, *"On earth as it is in heaven."* ***(Matthew 6:10)*** But overall 'as above so below' is a satanic philosophy used by Satan. The term 'As above so below' is used by occultists and it means that the marital world that is projected in the natural realm (or earth realm) comes from the marine kingdom (or as Christians like to call it, "Satan's kingdom!!!" Their job is to manifest Satan's kingdom in the earth realm and we clearly see that they're being successful in their establishment. Because this world is fallen and it can no longer mirror God or take on the image of God; instead this world mirrors and take on the image of Satan or the beast (666). Everything that we see in the natural is first taken place in the spiritual or in the deepest and darkest realm of Satan (which is below the earth realm). Everything that we see in the natural is the material world or as some would like to call it, "The Matrix!!!" is all an illusion to draw people into the pits of hell. *<u>The enemy doesn't come but to kill, steal, and destroy</u>*!!! ***(John 10:10)*** A lot of the things you want are satanic and they're there to lead you into the pits of hell. This is how the occultist walk by faith and not by sight because they completely understand that they're a part of a kingdom so they don't have to walk by the material world (or the earth realm) because they understand they they're the ones shaping the material world (and this is how Christians are supposed to be.) That's why I think that it's kind of foolish for Christians to purse these things here hoping that it's going to feel their void and add to their identity because it's not. Our identity is spiritual not physical because the kingdom of God is already at hand we just need to manifest it in the earth realm by listening to the Holy Spirit, taking what we see in the spirit according to what's in heaven (in the spiritual realm) and manifesting it in the earth realm. It's same thing with Moses when God told him to build the tabernacle ***(Exodus 25:1-9)*** *Then the Lord spoke to Moses, saying:* [2] *"Speak to the children of Israel, that they bring Me an offering. From everyone who gives it willingly with his heart you shall take My offering.* [3] *And this is the offering which you shall take from them: gold, silver, and bronze;* [4] *blue, purple, and scarlet thread, fine linen, and goats' hair;* [5] *ram skins dyed red, badger skins, and acacia wood;* [6] *oil for the light, and spices for the anointing oil and for the sweet incense;* [7] *onyx stones, and stones to be set in the ephod and in the breastplate.* [8] *And let them make Me a sanctuary, that I may dwell among them.* [9] *According to all that I show you, that is, the pattern of the tabernacle and the pattern of all its furnishings, just so you shall make it.* The people whom are in the world whom are spiritually blinded think that their identity comes from the physical when it's really a mirage of what's taken place in the spirit puffing up their pride and their sin nature in the natural because whether they believe it or not they're supporting the marine kingdom just by being an everyday sinner and supporting this demonic system that Satan has created. This is why the Lord tells you *to not be conformed to this world and be transformed by the renewing* *of your mind.* ***(Romans 12:2)*** I remember having a conversation with a sister in Christ over the phone about the things that goes on in her old state New Orleans. Her name was Brittney! She was telling me about the witchcraft and voodoo that's been going on around there that resulted in the murders, suicides, and high rate crime that goes on down there. She was telling me that they would practice ritual spells, blood sacrifices, incantations, and tarot cards (which are satanic). I was blown away because the media make it seem like New Orleans is just ratchet and ghetto but it's a spiritual war more than a physical war and this opened up my eye to the spiritual realm. When I was younger before I've got saved I tried doing a spell not knowing what I was doing and as a result of that some bad things had happened. One day when I went with my family coming from my grandmother's house after trying to perform a voodoo ritual from what I saw online and I felt like that was a gateway for the enemy to cause havoc and hell during that moment. Coming from my grandma's house it was on a three way intersection three cars had got into a bad wreck while we were at a stop light coming from my grandmother's house: One car was an red Chevy that spun out of control and flipped over while waiting at the stop light on the left side of our intersection, the second vehicle was an white GMC truck that went slamming into the third car moving out of their intersection while it wasn't their turn to go while the third car on the opposite side of the intersection tried turning our way going towards my grandmother's house from where we came from and the white GMC truck went crashing into the third vehicle leaving the people in the car severely injured and hurt. Now that I know what caused that tragic accident I repent of my wicked act and renounced any spells and hexes that I tried to put over my life or anyone else's life. Spiritual things aren't to be taken lightly especially when it comes to witchcrafts and spells. Coming to Christ I've had outer body experiences with the Lord and he even showed me the spiritual realm and the earth was nothing but darkness and full of demons. If anyone who's into new-age occultic philosophy I recommend that you stay away from stuff like that because God's hand isn't upon that kind of stuff. The world ***occult*** translated in Hebrew means *clandestine* **(done secretly)**, and hidden secrets. If it didn't come from God it's straight up witchcraft and it's from the devil because God and his kingdom have order; on the other hand, Satan and his kingdom doesn't because the bases of his satanic bible stems from the satanic philosophy "Do what thou wilt". Meaning there's no rules, do what you want to do, be your own god, you can get this power from the demonic realm but Satan knows they he doesn't have any real authority. If a witch was to cast a spell on an innocent person then God will have that curse come upon that witch tenfold because you reap what you sow. The Lord controls the peace and the evil and that is what Satan doesn't want these occultists to know. ***(Isaiah 45:****7)* *I form the light, and create darkness: I make peace, and create evil: I the Lord do all these things.* Jesus Christ is the head over all principalities and powers and

Satan can only go but so far. These occultists astral project into different dimensions in the spiritual realm because Satan teaches them that and they open themselves up to demonic possession and a lot of spiritual knowledge of good and evil that the Lord doesn't allow us Christians to know about. For those who don't know what astral projection is astral projection is a term used in esotericism to describe a willful out-of-body experience (OBE), a supposed form of telepathy, that assumes the existence of a soul or consciousness called an "astral body" that is separate from the physical body and capable of travelling outside of it throughout the universe as long as the spiritual umbilical cord is attached to the person's body this is referred to new agers as a sense of an "higher self" when really it's demonic because if you're not saved and you decided to astral project you are more than likely entertaining a familiar demonic spirit from lower demonic dimensions in the underworld of Satan and not the Holy Spirit because the Holy Spirit comes from above (which is in the heavens) and sinners don't have access to God because they have to first go through the son (which is Jesus Christ) to go to the father in order to gain a real sense of spiritual elevation so Satan can only give you a counterfeit version of an "higher self". When people astral project they can open up the door for demonic possession and if you're not saved demons can possess your whole body but if you're a Christian then demons can only demonize your soul because you're possessed by the Holy Spirit.

Any part of a Christians soul that isn't sanctified then that part of the soul is an open doorway for Satan and his demons that's why it's important for Christians to feel themselves us with the word of God. If we backslide, then we invite demons to torment us seven times more than before. When demons possess your soul they're possessing your will, mind, and emotions the question is what is Satan after, your mind. It's different when demons are possessing your flesh and flesh in the Greek means *sarkikos* meaning earthly and carnal you just have to renounce it and rebuke it then I would get in the word to make your flesh subject to your spirit man (which is the Holy Spirit). When demons control your mind, they are controlling your control box and you'd have to seek deliverance from a powerful deliverance minister in order to get delivered. (I wouldn't recommend astral projection to Christians because that's satanic and it can mess up your walk with the Lord nor am I going to tell you how to do it just don't do it because if you do it then you're out of God's boundaries and demons can cut your spiritual umbilical cord and take you straight to hell and demonize your body so don't do it I'm warning you.) Now that we've gotten that out of the way let's talk about spiritual spouses. (This is a rerun from my third book). Spirit Spouses are the most common thing in the dream realm (really known as the spiritual realm.) especially for people who engage in illegal sexual immorality. Spirit spouses are incubus and succubus spirits. ***Incubus spirits*** *(That attack females in their sleep)* are spirits that lies with people in their sleep; especially one that has engaged in sexual intercourse with someone illegally while they're sleeping. A ***Succubus spirit*** *(that attacks males)* is a demon transforming into a female or someone you're familiar with to get you to engage to have sex with them in your sleep. These demons are primarily spirits of sexual perversion. These demon spirits enter you through sexual intercourse to keep you bound and controlled to the devil. When you have sex, masturbate, watch pornography, or have oral sex you are not only opening up a doorway for those spirits to sexually harass you in your sleep but you've also formed a covenant with the demonic realm. Sexual immorality is a demonic sex ritual point blank period and once you engage in it you have formed a covenant with Satan and that spirit spouse. People are ignorant of this fact when they engage in illegal sex but Satan and his demons aren't. Ask me how I now, because I was once of those young teenagers who was addicted to pornography and masturbation and Lord knows the struggle was real but I didn't know the spiritual realm was real because I started doing it at thirteen and that was before I got saved and came into the knowledge of the truth. I've gotten saved at the age of seventeen and I've gotten my deliverance from pornography and masturbation addiction at the age of twenty but overall, I've been struggling with that addiction for seven years. On the day that I've gotten delivered from that addiction I've arrived at my grandmother house about to get ready for work I walked through the front door, cutting through the living room and walked pass in the hallway with a demonic rush passing my grandmother in the kitchen not saying anything to her I walked in the back of my uncle's Red room and jumped inside the bed. My grandmother called my name, "Xavier!!!" She asked!!! During my demonic phase, I chose not to answer her and I chose to go to sleep because of the oppression that the demon had on me was so strong that I was shaking, my body had a weird dark sensation all over my body especially my mind, I felt dead spiritually, my mind was numb, and I had a seizure on my uncle's bed but I recovered quickly so that I could go to my grandmother for deliverance. I got up but I was tip-toing towards the kitchen walking in the hallway slowly and as I approached her I couldn't talk because it was painful to speak and the demon that took over me wouldn't allow me to speak. So from my grandmothers point of view when I approached her and began to look at her my eyes started to roll in the back of my head and it was like I couldn't control it and she caught on to what that demon was trying to do and she quickly got up and got her anointed oil from her purse. As she begins to grab her anointed oil from her purse I ran back to my uncle's room and fell on the floor and about time she got towards me she touched my forehead and commanded that demon to come out of me and jumped up and fell to my knees again. Having a dark feeling or sensation leaving my body I still felt shaken by that spirit because it was that strong but not stronger than the blood of the lamb. Ya boy was struggling!!! She told me to call on the name of Jesus and I did and that helped with the rest of the demonic baggage that I was feeling and I felt all of it was gone. After that I decided to lay down and get some sleep but after I had experience a demon getting casted out of me I decided not to go to work that day because I felt sick and disgusted with myself and I felt ashamed and embarrassed, so I called off of work, repented to God and went to sleep feeling relived of my deliverance from that demon. Spirit spouses become more powerful when they successfully get you to have sex with them in a dream that you had. Often after you've woken up from such a lustful dream you may experience spiritual dryness, no presence of the Holy Spirit, and you may experience pain in your private part due to that spirit spouse harassing you sexually in a dream that you had. (Personally, I've experienced all three of those spiritual symptoms but the worst symptom for me was the spiritual dryness.) Like I felt like God was mad at me or I felt that I've grieved the Holy Spirit when I felt dry spiritually and I hated that because God's presence means everything to me and Satan knows that if he can lower your spiritual growth then he can torment you. Spirit spouses attack you the most especially if you're anointed by God and if you have a spiritual gift that he gave you through the Holy Spirit. They're going to attack you because they know that if they can suck your spiritual juice dry then you can't flow into the anointing that the Lord has given you that's why spirit spouses attack you sexually in your dream and want to have sex with you in a dream. The Jezebel spirit is a principality but not only that it's a spirit spouse. Jezebel's story can be found in 1st Kings and 2nd Kings, Jezebel was the daughter of Ethbaal, king of Tyre/Sidon, the priest of the cult Baal (*which was an occult revolting false God worship involved in sexual degradation and lewdness.*) Jezebel was married to a cowardly husband named Ahab which he was the king of Israel and he led the nation to worship the false demon god Baal ***(1st Kings 16:31)*** Elijah was a prophet from God and was sent out from the Lord to go kill Jezebel because of her rebellion against the Lord and her false god worship, she wanted the people of Israel to worship the false god Baal. She didn't repent of her sins so the Lord was going to bring judgement on her which the Lord had send Elijah to kill Jezebel. Jezebel was Elijah's enemy and she would pray death on him so when it was time for Elijah to kill Jezebel he fled from her because Jezebel threaten to kill him like she did to other prophets of God. So, after he fled, he plead for the Lord to kill him. ***(1st kings 19:1-4)*** Elijah had failed the assignment but one man wasn't scared of Jezebel and his name was Jehu. Jehu was another prophet from God but he got the job done that time. So, Jehu had caught Jezebel off guard and killed her while she was putting on makeup. ***(2nd Kings 9:30-37)*** The Jezebel spirit is not only about a woman being controlling over a man or a woman being dominating over the household there's many layers to the Jezebel spirit because she has multiple characters and her main goal is to get you trapped in a spider web and her biggest mind control tactic is manipulation, harassment, and doublemindedness. I could go on and on about the Jezebel spirit but I want to stay on topic about the spiritual spouse first. Spirit spouses can also cause late marriages and wedding delay's because you're still in covenant with them. Spirit spouses are the most common demons in the religion of shamanism because of their recent appearances in people's dreams due to sexual immorality Spirit spouses help shaman who assist them in their work, and to help them gain power in the world of spirit. Shamanism is basically a religion practiced by indigenous peoples of far northern Europe and Siberia that is characterized by belief in an unseen world of gods, demons, and ancestral spirits responsive only to the Shamans. The term "shamanism" was first applied by western anthropologists as outside observers of the ancient religion of the Turks and Mongols. Of course, if you're a Christian and have the Holy Spirit God will make you aware of these things because he can see the spiritual realm but we can't. People who believe in shamanism have half of the truth and I doubt that people who believe in that religion are Christians because when they come into the knowledge of the truth they are going to be some lit Christians for the kingdom of God because they're already aware of the spiritual realm and things like that. I bet you shamans have more information and knowledge about spirits and demons than churchianity and some Christians. Shaman's have had experiences in the spiritual realm but I doubt that they got that experience from the Lord mostly it's from a demonic spirit and they probably had to go through demonic initiation like the Illuminati and freemasons to enter into the spiritual realm.

We need the Lord in order to walk into the spiritual realm without getting torn into pieces by demons. When people are astral project little do they know that they're opening themselves up to demonic influence and demonic possession. I remember when a couple of brothers and sisters in Christ had emailed me about astral projecting. One sister in Christ had told me through an email that when she was experiencing astral projection she was trying to sleep and during her sleep state she was half awake but not fully awake and when she was sleeping she could feel her body moving. After she woke up from her sleep she told me that she felt disgusted and like she just got raped, I told her that it was probably a hallucination and a spirit spouse and she replied that it wasn't hallucination she said that it probably was a spirit spouse. Afterwards she thanked me and before we stopped talking she told me that she studied two years of psychology and that it was a false doctrine and later on she found out that psychology was dealing with some occultism stuff. When I heard her say that I thought to myself "because Satan knows how the human mind works because he's been mind screwing people for years." So basically, he builds religion based on what he knows because the Lord did condemn Satan but what the Lord didn't do was take away his knowledge. The reason for this is because the Lord already knew what was going to happen in the mist of Satan's harden heart so he had no choice but to condemn him out of the kingdom of heaven. Yes, Satan has knowledge but since his heart was corrupt and evil his knowledge and

everything that he knows about heaven is corrupted as well. The Lord turned him from a vessel of honor to a vessel of dishonor for the Lord's purpose. Demons have the knowledge of God as well but it's corrupt because Satan is their main leader as a vessel of dishonor and their goal is to blind the masses and test their loyalty towards God.
This is what you're seeing in today's society because majority of the people are blinded and sensitized. Spirit spouses is one of Satan's favorite demons to use on the masses because of their frequently activity in sexual immorality. Sex is like Satan's cheap instrument to use to control the masses of people because he wants them to get a soul tie with different people so that the soul can be fragmented and when the soul gets fragmented he can break down their mind and gain access to their mind and true Christians know what it feels like for a demon to have access to your mind. It's a nightmare!!! Spirit spouses can enter through watching pornography, lust, sexual immortality, evil dedication of individual, underwear manipulation, and through tattooing and incision. A spirit spouse isn't necessarily a female spirit, because spirits don't really have a gender. Gender basically serves a biological function: not a spiritual one. These spiritual spouses take on female gender in order to be more effective at bringing much damage and harm into men's lives. A spirit wife is just a feminine manifestation of the spirit husband phenomenon. Just like there are succubus (female-like) spirits. A spirit wife or succubus spirit will manifest through its male victim in the

form of extreme jealousy whenever he's in a relationship with a woman driving any woman away so that he can never maintain a long term healthy relationship and in the mist of that the man might experience rejection and due to it that may open up the door for the Jezebel sprit to come in which the man now has to deal with the spirit spouse, the Jezebel spirit, and the spirit of rejection I call it the triple threat match or handicap match against those spirits (I used to watch WWE wrestling back in the day when I was young so never mind me.) Anybody who's struggling to keep a job, joblessness, bad luck in business, or never really getting anything good financially off of the ground without great opposition he/she is most likely have a spirit spouse and their goal is to get you alone and by yourself and that goes for the same thing with the Jezebel sprit and the spirit of rejection that's why I call them the triple threat because all three of those spirits kind of have the same agenda which is to get you isolated. When a man or woman masturbate, that spiritual spouse will drive them to life of feeling ashamed and isolated. Before he/she engages in watching pornography that spirit may force that person to watch pornography or to participate in the demonic ritual. I've experienced a point to where that spirit spouse would speak to my flesh and it would say things like this, "You like that woman don't you?" or "You should out to masturbate to that porn you watched earlier." And then after you do it they'll accuse you and they'll tell you, "Look at you, you're pathetic!" "No woman will ever want you because you're struggling with lust or struggling with masturbation." That spirit will lead you towards having suicidal thoughts and maybe lead you to suicide. That's why I say every thought isn't your thoughts and you need to cast down every thought that goes against the spirit of the Lord and bring it back to captivity. ***(2nd Corinthians 10:5)*** Every time I went to sleep in my bed I have a random encounter with a spirit spouse and nine times out of ten it was in a form of some female that I knew or had a crush on and that spirit would drag me towards it and harass me sexually so that I can form a demonic covenant with it. Satanist know half of the stuff that we don't know about and if you look up the Satanist Aleister Crowley. Aleister Crowley basically engage in sex rituals more than any demonic rituals he's engaged in. He would participate in sex orgies and have sex with animals because that's what they do and that's how Satanist get down. Satanist doesn't see Satan the way that Christians see Satan because in their world they believe Satan is the real god and the heavenly father whom created heaven and earth is the restricting God. They have doctrines and scriptures like us but Satan describes himself as an angel of light or the true god to Satanist because he gives them knowledge and wisdom. Versus the true God that we serve (in their eyes) are a restricting God and he hates to see us grow and enhance and Satan is the truth. No wonder why when Satan told Eve that if she bit the forbidden fruit she would have all knowledge like God or be like God. ***(Genesis 3:4-5)***

And that's what Satanist believe but the Lord told Adam and Eve not to eat the forbidden fruit and if they did they shall surely die. ***(Genesis 2:16-17)*** The scriptures that Satan doesn't want you to know is those two scriptures which are in the beginning of the bible and Revelation chapter twelve in verse nine which explains the devil's defeat for deceiving the whole world: *So the great dragon was cast out, that serpent of old, called the Devil and Satan, who deceives the whole world; he was cast to the earth, and his angels were cast out with him.* ***(Revelation 12:9)*** The Lord is the way, the truth, and the life and nobody comes to the father but by through Jesus Christ our Lord and savior. ***(John 14:6)*** This is why some Satanist won't be able to come to the faith or the knowledge of the truth because Satan has already convinced them that they are gods and that Satan is the true god. They read scriptures just like us and it has the same effect on their "spirit" just like us but it's really a demonic spirit that's working in Satanists because they've been initiated into the marine kingdom. The bible says that in the last days men will be their own gods and lovers of themselves which is in second timothy in chapter three. People are manifesting the nature of Satan and they don't even know it because the whole point of what Satan is trying to do is get people to believe that they're gods and that they don't need a Lord and savior because they've got materialistic things. Now that you see the parallel between the kingdom of the Lord versus the kingdom of Satan you can rest in that revelation that we don't wrestle against flesh and blood but against principalities, powers, against the rulers of the darkness of this world, and against spiritual wickedness in high places. ***(Ephesians 6:12)***

CHAPTER EIGHT

The Anti-world

[2ND Timothy 3:1-7] "*This know also, that in the last days
perilous times shall come.*
2 *For men shall be lovers of their own selves, covetous,
boasters, proud, blasphemers, disobedient to parents,
unthankful, unholy,*
3 *Without natural affection, trucebreakers, false accusers,
incontinent, fierce, despisers of those that are good,*
4 *Traitors, heady, highminded, lovers of pleasures more than
lovers of God;*
5 *Having a form of godliness, but denying the power thereof:
from such turn away.*
6 *For of this sort are they which creep into houses, and lead
captive silly women laden with sins, led away with divers
lusts,*
7 *Ever learning, and never able to come to the knowledge of
the truth.*" (KJV)

When reading Mark 13:3-4 Jesus went to go sit upon the mount of the olives over against the temple, Peter, James, John, and Andrew asked Jesus what shall be the sign when all of these things (end time prophecy) occur. Then Jesus tells them from Mark 13:5-27 the signs of his second coming, then he tells the four disciples that no man knows the return of Jesus Christ but the Father in Mark 13:32.

In Mark 13:14 Jesus tells his disciples that when they see the abomination of desolation spoken of by Daniel the prophet in Daniel 9:27 to flee and he's referring to the Anti-ruler (Antichrist) that's going to make a covenant with Jerusalem after they rebuild the Jewish temple, destroy the people in the city of Jerusalem and the sanctuary then the anti-ruler (aka: The Anti-Christ Obama) will rule over them and claim to be god prior to the 2000 years before the actual prophecy occurs. So, Jesus was making a reference towards the future Anti-Christ not the Anti-Christ of their generation because there was already an Greek ruler during 167 B.C before Jesus came by the name of Antiochus Epiphanies who led over the temple of Jerusalem. So basically, Jesus was making a reference to the modern-day Antichrist who is Obama. Jesus told his disciples to basically don't worry about their home, materialistic items, or anything else but to take up their garments and flee when the Antichrist shows as Obama who will claim to be Jesus Christ, and many shall worship him. That's why Jesus warns us about the coming of many false Christ's and false prophets in these last days according to Mark 13:22. Test their Spirit!!! This is how you know if someone's of God or not what fruit of the Spirit are they bearing? Line it up with scripture: (Galatians 5:22-23) fruits of the spirit, (Galatians 5:19-21) and the lust of the flesh. This goes for other "Christians", friends, Obama and whatever you want to call it test the spirits. You shall know them by their fruits (Matthew 7:15-20).

The reason why the Lord said that he will turn those over to a strong delusion so that they may believe a lie is because they hate the truth. (2nd Thessalonians 2:10-12) *"And with all deceivableness of unrighteousness in them that perish; because they received not the love of the truth, that they might be saved.*
11 And for this cause God shall send them strong delusion, that they should believe a lie:
12 That they all might be damned who believed not the truth, but had pleasure in unrighteousness." (KJV) They love sin more than righteousness, they hated truth when God tried to correct them through Christians, videos, messages, songs etc. So basically, God turned them over to a reprobate mind so that they can no longer perceive the truth from God this goes for sinners and lukewarm Christians as well. The bible says that *it's better to be hot or cold than to be lukewarm because if you're lukewarm the Lord will chew you up and spit you out of his mouth* (Revelation 3:15-16). What are the signs of a lukewarm Christian:

1. You never read your bible aka the word of God: (you're Spirit man/women needs the fuel that it needs for God to operate through you and transform you and without the word of God your flesh overcomes your spirit because you're not programming your soul to transform into the image of Christ and when you're feeding your carnal man and not denying yourself your Spirit man/women is dying and your sinful desires manifest because you're not feasting on the word of God because the word of God is what transforms you.)
2. You're not fellowshipping with the Lord daily and you never spend any amount of time with him. (You must stay connected to the vine so that you can bear fruit and the vine is Jesus Christ and without you communing with Jesus you can't bear fruit of the Spirit in order to be transformed into his image.)
3. You look like the world: (What I mean by looking like the world I mean inwardly not outwardly because God doesn't look at the outward appearance he looks at the heart. What I mean by you resembling the world I mean by your character traits, your speech, how you carry yourself, how you respond to situations are they Christ like or are their worldly? If you ask yourself "Would Christ act like this, say this, behave like this." Etc. if not then stop doing it because in order to follow Jesus and make it into the kingdom we must deny out fleshly desires and bad and carnal family traditions that was instilled in us when we were in the world to take up the ways of Jesus in order to demonstrate the kingdom of God within us by walking in the Spirit and not fulfilling the lust of the flesh.

4. You listen to secular music and not Christian music that glorifies the Lord our God. This pertains to any kind of music that doesn't glorify God especially if it has cussing inside of it because people don't know that when you listen to a lot of rap artist who are cursing they're repeating and chanting incantations to you when they're rapping meaning they're releasing curses over your life to spell bound you and to bring havoc and chaos into your life if you're a Christian listening to stuff like that you need to repent and delete that stuff that doesn't glorify the Father. That also goes for Christian music that sounds like and resembles the world and this goes for old school samples put in gospel songs, melodies, and beats that Christian's try to Christianize because they're under grace but grace changes us and makes us new and that goes for the same thing when it comes to Christian music the Holy Spirit isn't going to bless something from the world and fit it into a Christian song when you were fornicating to the same song that you was listening to while you were in the world before you got saved (Ex: Kirk franklin, Marvin Sapp, Erica Campbell, Detrick Haddon etc.) Those are the artists that love to mix the clean with the unclean and God makes all things new according to (2nd Corinthians 5:17). Not saying that some Christian rappers are legit but somethings wrong when we take something from the world and try to sanctify it and we use grace as an excuse that goes for the same thing when it comes to pagan holidays, some Christians try to sanctify pagan holidays that God never told us to celebrate because most of these

pagan holidays that we celebrate came from the Roman catholic church and were connected to false Baal gods (but that's an whole other topic!!!) The point I'm trying to make is that you can listen to Christian rap it's nothing wrong with it (I'm a Christian music producer so I know the limits when it comes to making Christian rap) you can create your own beat just don't have it pattern after the samples of this world because that will be mixing the clean with the unclean.

5. You're ashamed to talk about Jesus and your faith in Jesus Christ. Jesus said to his disciples in Matthew 10:33, *"But whosoever shall deny me before men, him will I also deny before my Father which is in heaven."* You can also deny Jesus by not correcting someone when they're misusing scripture and trying to twist scripture to accommodate their sin and traditions but you know what they're saying isn't true correction is necessary if someone is misusing scripture.

Any sinner/ Lukewarm Christian who doesn't like rebuke, correction, repentance, but love to stay in sin the Lord will turn those over to a strong delusion because they rejected the truth (Romans 1:28-32).

The reason why many will bow down and worship the Antichrist is because for one they hate the truth and second, they suffer from a lack of knowledge. Hosea 4:6 tells us that the Lord's people suffer from a lack of knowledge. Probably because they're either ignorant or they're in sin. The bible says that the wages of sin is death (Romans 6:23). When Adam and Eve sinned they no longer could comprehend the things of God because the devil convinced them that if they eat the forbidden fruit that they would know good and evil just like God not knowing that when they ate it they awaken to their carnal senses and the natural realm to trade in their spiritual senses to the devil so they can no longer perceive the things of God because they became carnal and wanted the knowledge of good and evil over the knowledge of God and the tree of life. That's why the bible says in (Romans 8:6) that *"the carnal mind is death, but the Spirit of God is life and peace."* People who are in sin don't know the things of God because they've been cut off from him. That's why when you talk about the illuminati, the fore founders of the USA being freemasons, the election is fake etc. they discard it as a conspiracy because the carnal mind is **enmity** (opposed or hostile against something or someone especially against God. *Romans 8:7*)

Satan's goal is to create a satanic modern day utopian society!!! Trump is propagating to America and the whole world that he's an Christian when he goes to a roman catholic church where the pope worships the statue of Mary and he's a freemason as well. Trump says that he's going to make America great again which he's not it's all a part of the plan to cause chaos and confusion and I'll tell you how in a little bit. People hate Trump because he's horrible at being a president while at the same time professing to be a "Christian"!!! Check this out, when people see that he's an Christian running the office they're going to think that he's being a Christian is weak because Trump is coming in the name of Christ trying to make America great again. When People see America fall they're going to give up on Trump and Christ and start persecuting Christians then this is when Obama portrays himself as the savior of the world/nation. Obama comes back, ushers a global government known as the one world order aka the New world order and he saves the whole world through global assistance. Then he recommends that all religions come together when the Lord told us to be separate making all religions equal (2nd Corinthians 6:17) they're going to usher in a new financial plan which is to stop using dollar bills as an currency and he's going to usher in the mark of the beast making the poor and rich equal to one another, no more following the ten commandments but enforcing the new rules which is "Do what thou wilt" basically Obama is going to enforce communism the same way Hitler tried to enforce communism but he failed because the word of God says the Antichrist is coming by the way of peace not war and Hitler tried to force communism by war. Satan's going to come as an angel of light like the bible says as a way of peace.

Then Obama is going to reveal that he's god when he's not and he's going to throw away the bible, claim that it's not real and everyone do what they want to do. Another way that people are going to worship the Anti-Christ is he's going to do a whole lot of false signs and wonders and he's going to deceive the very elect and that's what Matthew 24:24 says when the Antichrist comes he's going to perform many false signs and wonders and deceive the very elect because of people's ignorance to the truth they're going to think that Satan is God when he cause the image of the beast to raise up and come alive by the power and the spirit of divination and sorcery and that is how he's going to finally convince that he's god when he's not and he's going to have the people take the mark of the beast to finally seal them as his people (when the people who really take the mark of the beast is doomed to hell for eternity according to Revelation 14:9-10) This is the big test the Lord's going to test us within these last days so we better get ready NOW!!!

A lot of "Christians" who claim to be Christians are going to accept the mark of the beast. The reason for this is because many of them are already indoctrinated with false doctrine as it is and they're already taught by the carnal religious church system about prosperity (which is a false sense of prosperity.) and they teach Christians to store up your treasures on earth and not in heaven, this is an direct contradictory towards the Lord's word according to ***(Matthew 6:19-21)*** where he says, *"Do not lay up for yourselves treasures on earth, where moth and rust destroy and where thieves break in and steal; [20] but lay up for yourselves treasures in heaven, where neither moth nor rust destroys and where thieves do not break in and steal. [21] For where your treasure is, there your heart will be also."* The reason why the Lord told us to do so is because he knows that the things of this earth are temporary and it's going to cause a stumbling block when it comes to your relationship with him. The Lord doesn't want the world capturing our heart to the point where we can't be obedient to him because we want so many materialistic things here. This will cause a lot of carnal Christians to take the mark of the beast because they're walking after their flesh instead of the spirit. Another reason why he tells us to store up our treasures in heaven is because he wants us to rest from our labor so that we can grow in faith when it comes to him and his provision for us because when the tribulation period kicks in it's going to be hard for Christians to let go of this world because we feel obligated to be a part of this demonic Babylonish system. The Lord hates obligation and it's completely opposite of his nature. When we stop and trust in God for our main provision then that's when we rest in his grace and we'll start to see blessings come down like crazy because he sees that you're no longer dependent upon the world to provide for you. When we labor and when we go outside of God to go pursue this job or this career, we are putting ourselves in bondage and under the **curse**. Especially if you're saving money and storing up treasures for yourself when the Lord told us not to do so. We put ourselves under the curse of God when we save money, when we put trust in man instead of God, when we sell things and when we buy things. Contrary to carnal Christians the Lord wants us to do the complete opposite. Don't save money ***(Matthew 6:19-21)***, don't put your faith in man but in the Lord ***(Jeremiah 17:5)***, don't sell things and buy things from other people for we are to freely give to one another as Christians ***(Matthew 10:8)***. The early church seemed to get the concept of freely giving and receiving more than us and we're the generation who have advanced technology. ***(Acts 2:45)*** The early church gave freely to each other because they understood that they're not under the tithes and offering law anymore better than we do. If we are continuing storing up treasures for ourselves and keeping it for ourselves instead of using it to help others then we cannot be fit to be Jesus's disciple. ***(Luke 14:33)*** *So likewise, whoever of you does not forsake all that he has cannot be My disciple.* This is one of the many things that we struggle with which is freely giving to one another. That is why the Lord is going to use the tribulation period to completely break us away from any crutch of money or materialistic items to bring us down to a place of humility so that we can finally freely give to one another and take care of the homeless just like he intended for us to do. The reason why a lot of Christians are going to fall away from the faith during the tribulation period is because they don't understand God's sovereignty and how he operates it's not just because we won't have money during the tribulation period it's because a lot of carnal Christians are destroyed for a lack of knowledge. If you're a carnal Christian then you'll be one of the many of them that's going to take the mark of the beast do you want to know why, because you're carnal and the carnal mind is at emity against God. ***(Romans 8:7)*** The carnal mind is a part of the flesh so you're going to walk according to the flesh if that's what you're operating under instead of the mind of Christ. The mark of the beast isn't just physical it's spiritual first!

Those who walk according to the flesh are going to walk according to the flesh and those who walk after the spirit will walk after the spirit. ***(Romans 8:5)*** The Greek word for the word *carnal* means ***sarkikos*** which then comes from the word ***sarks*** in the Greek which means flesh or fleshly.

The definition of the carnal mind is signified as having the nature of flesh i.e. sensual, controlled by animal appetites govern by human nature instead of the spirit of God. Those who aren't led by the spirit of God are carnal minded and fleshly minded. They have an animalistic nature to protect what's theirs and defend their territory like most animals do. Christians who are carnal minded not only act the way that the animals (whom I consider the sinners) who are still in the world act, but Christians who act like that are proven to be either double minded when it comes to God's word or they don't fully accept their identity in Christ. The beast is an animal and it walks according to its instincts and five senses; if something doesn't make sense according to its five senses it flips out and that's what a lot of carnal Christians do today. Animals who are still in the world whom are lost are already marked because they have an animalistic nature. This goes for sinners and carnal Christians! That is why the Lord puts us through trials and tribulations to sanctify use and purify us in order to transform us into the image of his son Jesus Christ, without sanctification then you won't be pure enough to go back home (which is heaven).

That is why he killed the old man in you and gave you a new nature in Christ because he wants you to make it into the kingdom of heaven. I know a lot of Christians don't want to see it that way but it's true. Our good is God giving us materialistic things but God's good is him shaping us into the image of his son so that we can enter into heaven without spot, wrinkle, or blemish. This is why he tells you to walk according to the spirit instead of the flesh because the flesh is damnation and it will lead you into the pits of hell if you're not properly abiding in Christ. Like I said, the mark of the beast is spiritual before it's physical and depending on which side your operating from: whether it be the flesh or the spirit. That'll determine whether or not you'll take the mark of the beast or endure till the end and go to heaven. Those who walk after the flesh are going to take it because they're bound to the things of this world and they hate righteousness and truth. Those who love truth, those who love conviction, and those who walk in the spirit will not fulfill the lust of the flesh because they've accepted this one truth: that they've been crucified with Christ through faith in the gospel. Without faith, you don't have salvation! Your faith is required in order to take ahold on what the Lord has promised you and that goes for anything else that the Lord has promise to give you as well including your salvation. If you didn't have faith in Jesus for your salvation then what's the point of you getting saved in the first place? The word says, *"Faith comes by hearing and hearing by the word of God."* ***(Romans 10:17)*** You have to hear the gospel in order to believe that goes along with you walking out your salvation with fear and trembling. Before you walk out your salvation you have to take ahold of it by faith and as you talk ahold of your salvation by faith God's going to give you the grace and power to walk out your salvation operating from the realm of faith. Faith and works go hand and hand you can't be a hearer of the word you have to be a doer as well. ***(James 1:22-23)*** You don't see that with a lot of Christians today, they just want to claim salvation without walking out their salvation while at the same still in the world, still remaining the same, not being conformed to the image of Jesus Christ where do you think that they're going? If they're not being sanctified, cleansed, purged of any fleshly desires, and they're lukewarm where do you think that they're going, to hell my friend. Your once saved always saved isn't true you have to be sanctified and purged of the old man in order to enter into the kingdom; no flesh, people whom are still bound to the flesh, and people whom are operating in the flesh are going to enter into the kingdom for ***(1st Corinthians 6:8-11)*** tells us so. Now that we've gotten that out of the way let's talk about the Anti-Christ. People who already have disregarded Jesus are already carrying the spirit of antichrist's in the world for the word tells us that in ***(1st John 2:18)***. All of these "celebrities" that people look up to are leading them into the pits of hell and the celebrities are preparing them for the Antichrist so that they can receive the mark of the beast. You can see one of Rihanna's Samsung commercial titled: Antidairy where she shows you the road to "success" in the entertainment industry. In the beginning, she wakes up in a bedroom filled with accessories for example, a piano, wooden horse, and many other things.) When she wakes up she sees two little children playing the piano and they are playing hind and go seek with Rihanna under the covers. The next thing you know the two little children walk backwards towards this open dark room where you can't see anything because it's pitched black. As Rihanna decides to follow the two little kids she noticed that there was a key on the floor with a written tag attached to the key named R8. Rhianna kneels down to pick up the key and she continues heading towards the dark room where the kids were heading at. As she proceeded to walk through the door to transition into another room, she notices a young version of herself with a crown over her eyes resembled a younger

Rihanna who wanted to become famous and make money. The next thing you know she walks into a studio where she does music and she starts playing with the mixing board and the next thing you know as she touches the mixing board she moves her body as if a demon had gone into her and possess her body twisting and twitching her body around as she become one with the music (I guess performing witchcraft over the music.) Next, she walks into another room where four waitresses approach her with measuring type trying to measure her body to see if she fit enough to go through the dark portal. After the four waitresses checked to see if Rihanna had fitted enough to go through the dark portal where her younger self was they decided to let her go through it. As she goes through the dark portal he whole image transform into this dark iconic singer that everyone idolizes and lust after. This signifies that she has become one with darkness and she's now living the fantasy dream that her younger self wanted to become. Next Rihanna enters into another room from what it looks like is a tattoo pallor. Rihanna walks in and sees a chubby guy sitting in the chair waiting to get tattooed. The guy with sitting in the chair hands her over the razor for her to tattoo him. She approaches the man in the chair and gets on top of him and starts marking his head with the mark of the beast that the book of revelations talks about. ***(Revelations 13:16-17) And he causeth all, both small and great, rich and poor, free and bond, to receive a mark in their right hand, or in their foreheads: [17] And that no man might buy or sell, save he***

that had the mark, or the name of the beast, or the number of his name. As she's marking him with the razor on his forehead the man sitting in the chair starts bleeding from the eyes, to his feet. This represents spiritual death and if you receive the mark of the beast you will be eternally damned into the pit of hell forever and ever. The man wakes up from the nightmare and recognizes that is was only just a dream. As he wakes up he notices that the nightmare was actually a reality and he got mad and started going crazy. Then when the guy turned around, he notices that a younger Rhianna was standing on top of the chair that he was sitting in with her arms folded as if she was disappointed in him for some reason. The next scene Rihanna is seen in a tub as she sits in the tub she notices as she looks around there are shadows or people behind the four corners of the wall watching her. This represents her handlers from the elite! As she notices that they're watching her she starts to dip her body in the tub causing only her head to be seen and as she's laying in the tub she comes back up and black ink is shown coming from the water this is a mockery of Jesus Christ! As she comes up, she recognizes her younger self fading away. This represents the baptism of the Anit-Christ, and her losing her younger self due to fame and fortune. Next Rhianna enters a room to where there are musicians or Satanist who lust after her as she walks through the door with them looking subdued by her charm as she walks from the aisle towards the stage. The seduced crowed follows her and ever steps she takes they move along with her and every stop she takes the crowd stops with her. As she enters the stage the crowd drop like flies and when they wake up her younger self appears in the room again with the crown still over her eyes then a younger version of Rhianna walks out of the room. Next Rihanna enters the room where money is kept and the women sitting at her desk shows her the bank room where the Zionist keep control of the money. On the lady's desk, there's a Baphomet symbol on her desk and there's an Egyptian pyramid on his desk this represents the illuminati or the elite. As Rhianna walks towards the safe and opens up the safe she saw elderly people typing up something that looks like a long receipt or something. Then she walks out of the safe and closes it afterwards only to be reconcilliating with her younger version of herself to receive a crown. After she receives the crown she pops up in a dark room! Then another scene pops up to where the Zionist are continuing typing in the safe as usual and then a person dies in the safe while typing. The others who were typing just looks at the corpse like the person was nothing but an instrument used to corrupt the masses and they replaced the corpse with a fresh Zionist like it was nothing that just goes to show you how wicked this world really is. As Rhianna walks back into her room she uses the key that she first found on the floor during the beginning of the video to open the door as she opens the door and walks through the door she realizes that the same people who were standing with her to go escort her to the stage was in the same room that she was in from the very beginning of the video. The room that once was full of life was full of death and nothing seemed alive anymore as sand was covering the room symbolizing the spiritual death that fame and fortune gave her in the result of her selling her soul to the devil. As Rhianna approaches her bed she realizes that the two kids that disappeared during the beginning of the video was knocked out sleep in her bed. She then lays down on her bed to go to sleep! Before she goes to sleep, she looks up at a light in the sky hoping someone comes towards her rescue. That just goes to show you that the bible is true. ***(John 17:17)*** *For what does it profit a man to gain the whole world and lose their own soul?* ***(Mark 8:36)*** This is God's way of showing his children that nothing in the world is eternal and it's temporary. You can see that with Solomon in the book of Ecclesiastes from chapter one through two. God allowed Solomon to gain all of that wisdom, knowledge, and material stuff to show he that it's all vain without God. *There's no new thing under the sun!* ***(Ecclesiastes 1:9)*** These occultists that try to gain "spiritual enlighten" through the devil and they've bitten from the tree of good and evil instead of going to the tree of life (which represents God) to gain information. If people tried it in the biblical days so can people try it in the modern days it's still going to bring the same unfulfillment and dissatisfaction. We were made for God and for his purpose only and to find identity in materialistic things, people, and careers then we're really stripping ourselves of our true identity when only our true identity can come from the Lord our God. Nothing's going to last, it's all going to perish and it's all going to burn up according to revelations so it doesn't even matter. On the other hand, you're eternal so I suggest you make up your mind to find out if you want to serve God or serve mammon and materialistic things that won't matter in the near future. It's up to you!

CHAPTER NINE

The coming of our Lord and Savior

Some churches believe in the pre-tribulation rapture and the pre-tribulation rapture is a man-made doctrine where it talked about Jesus coming to rescue us before the tribulation period and leaving some Christians behind and coming back on his second coming to pick up the remnant Christians and to destroy the earth that is false doctrine according to ***(Matthew 24:29-31)*** which explains that we are taken up by Jesus after the tribulation period not before the tribulation period because the second coming and the rapture are the same things but Christians try to make the two words different meanings to deceive themselves into believing that the second coming and the rapture are two different things but the rapture and the second coming is the same thing so they suppress the truth in unrighteousness because they hate righteousness therefore leading thousands of souls astray. This is coming from my own mouth, ***"We will be here to face the tribulation period!"*** The pre-tribulation doctrine was made up to accommodate the scary westernize Christians who are scared to face the tribulation period and Christian persecution because they want to save their life's instead of losing their lives for Christ names sake. Christians on the eastern side of the globe already are experiencing persecution day after day and will die behind what they believe in but because you have materialistic Christians on the western side of the globe being taught a lot of false doctrine and modern-day gospel sermons that don't feed them the meat of the gospel Christians like American Christians aren't expecting to undergo any persecution because they listen to the filth that they watch on television instead of getting into their bible and learning the word of God for themselves by the counsel of the Holy Spirit, these are the Christians that are lukewarm and only accept the watered down gospel which is also known as the prosperity gospel and to name a few apostate preachers one is Creflo Dollar, Joel Osteen, and T.D. Jakes. These are the apostate preachers who hold back the truth because of their unrighteousness leading thousands of souls astray due to their prosperity gospel having people believe that if you sow a $100.00 seed you'll get $10,000.00 back, I see a new house, new car, I see a wife/husband on the way etc. because they have to create a false Christlike doctrine that's going to appeal to the flesh, the ego, the carnal westernize church, and the world because they know that Americans are very proud and materialistic so they cook up another Jesus and another gospel and apostle Paul warns us about this in ***(Galatians 1:8)*** *But though we, or an angel from heaven, preach any other gospel unto you than that which we have preached unto you, let him be accursed.*

These prosperity pimps know that the real gospel of Jesus Christ isn't going to be appealing to folks because they know that the real gospel doesn't direct you towards here but the real gospel directs you towards heaven. Anybody who has been a representative or a witness for Jesus Christ (who was God in the flesh) got persecuted and beaten. If you look up the Greek word for the word "witness" it's translated in the Greek language as ***mártyras*** and the English translation from the word ***mártyras*** is called ***martyrdom*** which means suffering death because of one's religious beliefs. When you first get saved you've been crucified with Christ Jesus so this means that it's no longer you that lives but it's Christ who lives in you and you're seated in heavenly places with him and the reason for this is because he wants to manifest himself through you by using your bodily vessel in order to attract men to himself in order to get them saved so basically once you get saved you need to know that your will is gone so you don't have a say from now on for one and for two you will have to become an martyr for this gospel man because satan knows that because you've got God dwelling in you now (no matter what spiritual level you're on in the faith) he'll have to kill you because he sees the potential threat and damage that you can do this his kingdom in the earth realm and he don't want that so he'll do whatever is necessary to take you out. He (Satan) has been wanted to take you out way before birth because he knows what God has for you and he doesn't want you to become what the Lord has predestine you to become because he knows you'd be an potential threat towards Satan and his kingdom and this is why you were going through hell when you were born it's not God's fault it's Satan but God can use what Satan did and turn it around for your good if you let him and what you've gone through isn't even about you it's to help someone else who's struggling with the same thing that you struggled with in order to get that person saved or to plant an Godly seed inside of that person in order to get them saved so whatever the enemy does God turns it around for your good so that he can get the glory. Satan knows that his time is almost up that's why he's doing all he can do before the Lord comes back to wreck this hell hole. You have to be strong in the faith and endure to the end in order to be saved because this world is going to get worser and worser as time goes by don't be deceive by Donald Trump's promise to America that he's going to make America great again that's an lie from the pit of hell brethren and this is the scripture that the Lord gave me concerning the "peace" that Donald Trump is going to being to America. ***(1 Thessalonians 5:3)*** *"For when they shall say, Peace and safety; then sudden destruction cometh upon them, as travail upon a woman with child; and they shall not escape."* When people have been given truth about Trump, the Antichrist that will soon be coming to power, and the end times but they still want to turn away from it after the Lord has send that person multiple people to warn them about the times that we're in God will send that person a strong delusion that they might be damned because they had pleasure in unrighteousness. ***(2nd Thessalonians 2:11)*** *"For when they shall say, Peace and safety; then sudden destruction cometh upon them, as travail upon a woman with child; and they shall not escape."*

This isn't funny your soul and eternal destination is at stake you can play with your life if you want to when you die you shall appear at the judgement seat of God and be judged to whether you go to heaven or hell and if you're not saved you're going straight to hell but if you're saved and you continued pressing in the Spirit of God and you die a solider and not in your sins you go straight to heaven after you die being a solider in the Lord's army you don't go to heaven or hell base on your own works and righteousness because your works are as filthy rags unto the Lord because no one is righteous outside of Christ, we are saved by grace through faith in the gospel and the resurrection of our Lord and savior Jesus Christ not by our works and self-willed efforts. So, you have to make sure your heart is right with the Lord and make sure that you're in the right place with him because no one else is going to be held accountable for what you did in your mortal body but you.

Printed in Great Britain
by Amazon